THE NEW MERMAIDS

Every Man in His Humour

THE NEW MERMAIDS

General Editors
PHILIP BROCKBANK
Professor of English, York University

BRIAN MORRIS
Lecturer in English, York University

Every Man in His Humour

BEN JONSON

Edited by MARTIN SEYMOUR-SMITH

ERNEST BENN LIMITED
LONDON

First published in this form 1966
by Ernest Benn Limited
Bouverie House · Fleet Street · London · EC4
© Ernest Benn Limited 1966
Distributed in Canada by
The General Publishing Company Limited · Toronto
Printed in Great Britain

CONTENTS

Acknowledgements   ix

Abbreviations Used in Notes   xi

Introduction   xiii

   The Author   xiii

   The Play   xv

Note on the Text   xxxii

Further Reading   xxxiv

EVERY MAN IN HIS HUMOUR   1

   The Dedication   3

   The Persons of the Play   5

   The Text   7

TO KEITH BRACE
WITH GRATITUDE

ACKNOWLEDGEMENTS

ANY JONSON editor's chief debt must be to Herford and Simpson's edition of Jonson's works. I have made extensive use of this. It superseded Simpson's earlier single volume edition of *Every Man in His Humour* (Oxford, 1919), which, however, I did consult—and which is still in print. Another valuable aid was H. H. Carter's accurate reprint of the Quarto and Folio texts in parallel (New Haven, 1921), with its extremely useful notes, now out of print and very difficult to obtain. Other editions consulted include those in: Lt. Colonel Cunningham's reprint of Gifford's edition of the *Works*, the standard edition before Herford and Simpson (London, 3 vols., 1871; 9 vols., 1875); B. Nicholson's 3 volume old Mermaid edition (1893–4); F. E. Schelling's *Complete Plays* (2 vols., Everyman's Library) contains a modernized version of the Quarto and is still in print; W. A. Neilson's *Chief Elizabethan Dramatists* (New York, 1911). The two single volume editions most consulted were: ed. G. B. Harrison, London, 1926 and ed. A. Sale, London, 1941 and 1963. I am grateful to the London Library and to the Bexhill branch of the East Sussex County Library (whose staff are so long suffering on my account) for finding me difficult and even apparently impossible books and articles. Brian Morris saved me from foolish errors and made wise suggestions. My wife's help with typing and other tasks was invaluable. I am also grateful to the printers, whose careful setting of the text made things as easy as possible.

Bexhill-on-Sea, 1 January, 1966.   MARTIN SEYMOUR-SMITH

ABBREVIATIONS USED IN NOTES

ed. = any editor at any time.

eds. = all (post 1716) editors.

Q = *Every Man in His Humour*, 1601.

F1 = text of EMiHH in *Workes*, 1616.

F2 = text in *Workes*, 1640.

F3 = text in *Works*, 1692 (reprinted 1716).

Ff = text common to all three Folios.

H & S = text in *Ben Jonson*, vol. III, edited C. H. Herford and P. Simpson, Oxford, 1927.

G = text in Lt. Colonel F. Cunningham's reprint of Gifford's edition of Jonson's *Works*, 1871.

Nn = text in old Mermaid ser. selection, edited B. Nicholson (introduction by C. H. Herford), 3 vols., 1893–4.

Sh = text of FI in Everyman ed. of Jonson's *The Complete Plays* ed. F. Schelling, 2 vols., 1910 (this also contains Q).

N = text in W. A. Neilson's *Chief Elizabethan Dramatists*, 1911.

H = ed. G. B. Harrison, 1926.

S = A. Sale (1941, 1963).

G+ = All editions since Gifford's.

INTRODUCTION

THE AUTHOR

BENJAMIN JONSON, known by his own preference and that of posterity as Ben, was born in 1572, probably on 11 June, in or near Westminster. He was the posthumous son of a Protestant minister; soon after his birth his mother married a bricklayer. He was sent to Westminster School, where his master was William Camden, the antiquary, to whom he dedicated *Every Man in His Humour*. Probably he did not finish at Westminster, but was removed by his stepfather about 1589 and apprenticed to the bricklaying trade. Gibes about this followed him to his grave, and do little credit to those who made them.

From 1589 until his appearance in Henslowe's *Diary* in 1597 little is known of him. He was in the wars in Flanders and killed an enemy in single combat, and he married, probably in 1594, a woman called Anne Lewis. A seven-year-old son died in 1603. It seems likely that after his career as a soldier he became an actor. From later references to him we gather that he was a strolling player in 1597, and that he played the part of Hieronimo in *The Spanish Tragedy*. He completed Nashe's lost play *The Isle of Dogs* (1597), which became the subject of legal proceedings for reasons not now clear. Nashe fled to Yarmouth, but Jonson was imprisoned for a time. He had written a number of plays by 1598, including some lost comedies and one tragedy. His career proper, as he himself conceived it, began with *Every Man in His Humour*, which was produced by the Lord Chamberlain's men with great success at the Curtain Theatre in September 1598 (perhaps because of a difference with Henslowe) with Shakespeare in the cast. Within a week or so of this event Jonson had a duel with one of Henslowe's actors, Gabriel Spencer, and killed him. He was branded as a felon but escaped hanging through the routine reciting of his neck-verse. While in prison he became a Roman Catholic, and remained one until 1610 (when he said he celebrated his return to the Anglican fold by drinking off the whole bottle of wine at Communion).

Between 1599 and 1601 Jonson was deeply involved in the complicated so called 'war of the theatres', between the select playhouses in the city and the public ones on Bankside. After a period of poverty, when he was supported by Sir Robert Townshend, and a failure in 1603 with the still underrated tragedy *Sejanus* (1603), Jonson became established and successful. His Catholicism seems to have had little effect on his career: he wrote a long series of masques and entertainments for the Court, and enjoyed some influence there. He and his wife were examined for recusancy in 1606, but this seems to have been a technicality, for in 1605 he had actually been employed by the government to discover the conspirators in the Gunpowder Plot. When in 1604 Marston and Chapman were imprisoned for making fun of James I (an occupation difficult to resist) in *Eastward Ho!*, in which he had also collaborated, he joined them voluntarily, and may have been instrumental in their all three avoiding the threatened penalty of having their noses slit. His finest plays, *Volpone*, *Epicene*, *The Alchemist*, followed in the next few years. In 1612 he went with Ralegh's son, as tutor, to the Continent. In 1616 was published the definitive Folio edition of his works: no English author before him had seen his own works through the press with such scrupulous care, nor had plays ever before been treated as seriously. It is unlikely that the Shakespeare Folio of 1623 would ever have been inaugurated had it not been for the prestige accorded to playwriting by Jonson by his inclusion of plays in his Folio volume. His is probably the greatest single influence on punctuation practice in the whole of English literature; authors gave little or no attention to the matter before him. The contribution made by this man, who never attended a university—though he later became an honorary M.A. of both— to the stature of poetry and to the prestige of the poet in society is impossible to estimate. In 1616 his supremacy as a professional man of letters was recognized by the granting to him of a pension of £66.13.4 (one hundred marks) a year for life.

During his last twenty-five years Jonson wrote fewer plays, and those he did write show some falling-off. *The Staple of News* (1626) is his last good play. In 1623 his library was destroyed by fire, which he lamented in his poem *An Execration Upon Vulcan*.

In 1628, at the age of fifty-six, Jonson had a stroke, and he appears to have been paralysed and confined to his room for the remaining nine years of his life. In this final period he wrote three poorish plays, *The New Inn* (1628/9), *The Magnetic Lady* (1632) and *A Tale of a Tub* (1633), which was perhaps a revision of a play originally written in 1596/7. He also wrote two masques for the Court of Charles I, and other entertainments. He seems to have been forgotten by some—but not by a whole generation of poets known as 'the Tribe of Ben' or 'Ben's boys'. There is no doubt that this group, which included almost every poet of talent (but not Milton) of the time, sincerely admired him, and cheered his last days. He died in Westminster on 6 August 1637, and was buried in the Abbey.

Jonson was an arrogant and quarrelsome man, who hardly courted popularity. That he was so respected is a tribute to the solidity of his achievement and to his essential warmth and humanity. The essence of his critical thought is to be found in *Timber: or, Dis-*

coveries; Made upon Men and Matter (1641). He has suffered, as has often been pointed out, by being so highly respected that he remains unread, as if his work were dry or boring. The monumental eleven-volume Oxford edition of his works by Herford and Simpson, and the spate of studies and articles that have followed it, are doing much to rectify this state of affairs. He is remembered and valued for his understanding of poets (such as Shakespeare and Donne) who were very different from himself, for his brilliant formulations of sound and practical critical principles, his genius for subtle and witty characterization, his magnificent craftsmanship in versification and dramatic structure, and, perhaps above all because permeating all his work and transcending his faults, his sound good sense.

THE PLAY

THE HISTORY OF THE PLAY

Every Man in His Humour exists in two forms: the Quarto version issued in 1601, and the revision which opens the 1616 Folio collection, hereinafter referred to respectively as Q and F. A notice inserted at the end of F states 'This comedy was first Acted, in the year 1598. By the then L. Chamberlain his Servants.', and lists Shakespeare, Burbage, Hemings and Cordell (the latter pair master-minded the Shakespeare Folio of 1623, perhaps with Jonson's active help and advice), among others, as 'the principal comedians'. This date for the first performance, which must have been at the Curtain Theatre, Shoreditch, is confirmed and further limited by a reference, preserved in F, to a Burgundian, John Barrose, who was hanged for murder on 10 July 1598 (IV, ii, 17), and by a letter from Toby Mathew to Dudley Carleton of 20 September 1598, in which he speaks of a German who lost 300 crowns at 'a new play called, Every Man's Humour'. There are some interesting references to the play made before its publication, which show that it was a success. In *Th' overthrow of Stage-Plays* (1599) a self-exiled Puritan, Richard Schilders, wrote of those who 'bring upon the Stage the very sober countenances, grave attire, modest and matronlike gestures and speeches of men and women to be laughed at as a scorn and reproach to the world' and went on to claim that his book had been issued 'to correct the bad humour of such humourists as these'. In 1601 another, unidentified, writer, W. I., not so offensively puritan, attacked Jonson in a book called *The Whipping of the Satire*.

There is a tradition, first recorded by Rowe in 1709, the details of which are suspect, but the main fact of which may well be true, that Shakespeare interceded on Jonson's behalf when his manuscript was on the point of being rejected. Evidently Shakespeare played the part of Old Kno'well.

The title *Every Man in His Humour* appears first in the Stationer's
Register in 1600 (its entry follows another of May 1600, and there
is no reason to doubt the date), when, along with *As You Like It*,
Henry V, and *Much Ado About Nothing*, it was entered 'to be
stayed': this almost certainly meant that Shakespeare's company
was insuring it against piracy by an unauthorized printer. Later in
the same year it was entered by Cuthbert Burby and Walter Burre,
and in 1601 Q made its appearance under the imprint of Walter
Burre, 'As it hath been sundry times publicly acted by the right
Honourable Lord Chamberlain his servants'. The printer is
unknown.

It has been demonstrated beyond doubt by Herford and Simpson
that F was set up 'from a copy of the 1601 Quarto which Jonson had
worked over with manuscript corrections to prepare it for the press'.
(The eccentric assertion of H. de Vocht, to the effect that Jonson
did not oversee the 1616 Folio, was totally destroyed by Herford and
Simpson, and can safely be ignored.) Q had been set ostensibly in
Florence, although it is clear that Jonson had even then conceived
his play against a backcloth of contemporary London. In his revision
he preserved the time, 1598, but changed the scene from an unconvincing Florence to a remarkably real and informative London. He
further improved the text by substituting the colloquial forms of
the contemporary stage (which he had done so much to develop) for
the literary dialogue of Q. The main differences between Q and F
are discussed in a later section.

As a stage-play *Every Man in His Humour* has hardly ever fallen
entirely out of fashion. Garrick 'improved' it in 1752, playing the
part of Kitely, but giving himself much additional dialogue and
cutting out large sections of the play that seemed irrelevant to his
own performance. As Theophilus Cibber observed, he gave the
original to his cat, and 'What Puss clawed off, the Actor left out'.
Dickens loved the play, and enjoyed acting the part of Bobadill, for
reasons that can easily be imagined. There have been several revivals
in this century, and the play is popular with amateurs.

THE DATE OF REVISION

Various dates have been put forward, but by far the most convincing
is that put forward by Simpson in his 1919 Oxford edition, and
adhered to by Herford and himself in their subsequent Collected
edition. There is every reason to suppose that Jonson began work on
the 1616 Folio in 1612, and since it was *Every Man in His Humour*
that was chosen to open the volume, it is likely that he undertook
the revision in this same year. The dates of 1601 and 1606 that
have been suggested are unconvincing if only in that there would
have been less pressing reasons for them—whereas in 1612 Jonson

would have had the incentive to prepare and drastically revise the play with which he had made his first reputation. We know that he thought of *Every Man in His Humour* as the foundation of his achievement from the *Induction* to *The Magnetic Lady* (1632), where he wrote of himself as 'beginning his studies of this kind, with every man in his Humour . . .'. The whole manner of the revision belongs to his mature period. The arguments for a date of 1601 do not really merit discussion, since they depend on the rather absurd basis that new references to the Queen would not have been introduced if so careful a recasting had taken place in the reign of James I. But it was utterly characteristic of Jonson to have revised the play to take place in a particular past year. Besides which, as Simpson pointed out, John Trundle (I, ii, 54) did not begin to publish until 1603.

The arguments for a date of 1606 cannot be dismissed quite so lightly, but they are unconvincing, if only because there is no evidence for a revival of the play in 1606, and because they depend on Jonson's having intended to bring the play up to date in that year—which he clearly could not have wished, since he introduced new references to the Queen and preserved others. These arguments are summarized and refuted by Simpson in his Introduction to his 1919 edition, which is reprinted more or less verbatim in the later (1927) Herford and Simpson Collected edition.

What will clinch the argument for 1612 for most readers is the introduction of two lines given to Kitely in III, ii:

He's no precisian, that I am certain of.
Nor rigid Roman Catholic. . . .

Jonson himself said that he remained 'twelve years' a Catholic after the killing of Spencer. Is it likely that, while a Papist, he would have put these words into Kitely's mouth? The notion that he was poking fun at the popular mistrust of Catholics seems beyond possibility; it would not have gone down with any audience; besides, as Simpson pointed out, 'Roman' has a marked Protestant ring.

All the real evidence, in fact, goes to support the theory that Jonson revised the text of Q in 1612, in order that it might take its place as the first of the plays in the collected edition that was almost certainly first planned in that year.

JONSON AND THE THEORY OF HUMOURS

The extent to which Jonson, in the composition of his earlier plays— notably *Every Man in His Humour*, *Every Man out of His Humour*, *Cynthia's Revels*, *Poetaster*—was guided by his theories concerning humours has not been, and perhaps never will be, determined. Certainly the question of humours has bedevilled discussion of these plays: critics of an earlier generation tended to look for 'humour theory' in them, and consequently to distort them. The truth is that Jonson chose to exploit a topic—'humours'—that was in the air, in order to express his own theories of drama; and further, as he developed as a dramatist, the achievement of his plays transcended theoretical considerations more and more frequently—a fact that is still not sufficiently acknowledged, in spite of the large number of books that have been written on him in recent years. Even Herford and Simpson, whose massive edition of his works has done so much to rehabilitate him, may have insisted too rigidly upon his originality as a theoretician, and thus sometimes tended to smother his dramatic and poetic achievement in a web of critical theory.

Neither the idea of humours nor, wholly, the comedy of humours was invented by Jonson. This was the old-fashioned assumption. By the time Jonson came to concern himself with the stage, the topic was so lucubrated that he could even satirize (at any rate by the time he came to write *Every Man out of His Humour*) a certain current fashionable use of the term 'humour': when it was used to describe a mere fad or affectation, such as the wearing of particular clothes, or a whimsicality of speech. This use had developed naturally from the Fourteenth Century use of the word to denote the supposed fluid constituents of the body. A fuller history of the word in this connection may be found in Charles Read Baskerville's *English Elements in Jonson's Early Comedy* (Texas, 1911) and in Simpson's Introduction to his edition of *Every Man in His Humour* (Oxford, 1919). Baskerville argued that Jonson had been deeply influenced in his thinking on the subject by his reading of Lyly, Nashe and of Fenton's *Tragical Discourses* (1567); Simpson snubbingly refused to accept this. Nevertheless, opinion is now perhaps swinging more towards Baskerville's thesis.

Medieval medicine associated physical and mental dispositions with the preponderance of certain humours in the body: blood (hot and moist), phlegm (cold and moist), yellow bile (hot and dry) and black bile (cold and dry) should blend equally in the body. Imbalance led to various kinds of distempers. The theory became more and more complex, and the most elaborate account is to be found in Burton's *Anatomy of Melancholy*, by which time, however, medicine had begun to discountenance the theory. As has frequently been pointed out, the notion was not as silly as it may sound to us today—most particularly in its insistence that every psychological disorder had its origin in a physiological one.

The use of 'humour' in the sense of 'mood' has been traced back at least to 1525: 'Hacklewitt and another . . . in a mad humour . . . coyted him . . . to the bottom of the stairs'. A few years later it could generally be understood to mean 'a particular disposition . . . especially one having no apparent ground or reason'. This is really the main use that was exploited by Jonson's predecessors, and it was fastened upon by Jonson himself. In the *Induction* to *Every Man out of His Humour* (1600), the first humour play he committed to the press, Jonson provided a clear definition of what he meant in the words of Asper, the presenter:

Why, Humour (as 'tis *ens*) we thus define it
To be a quality of air or water,
And in itself holds these two properties,
Moisture, and fluxure: as, for demonstration,
Pour water on this floor, 'twill wet and run:
Likewise the air (forc'd through a horn, or trumpet)
Flows instantly away, and leaves behind
A kind of dew; and hence we do conclude,
That whatsoe'er hath fluxure, and humidity,
As wanting power to contain itself,
Is Humour. So in every human body
The choler, melancholy, phlegm, and blood,
By reason that they flow continually
In some one part, and are not continent,
Receive the name of Humours. Now thus far
It may, by *Metaphor*, apply itself
Unto the general disposition:
As when some one peculiar quality
Doth so possess a man, that it doth draw
All his affects, his spirits, and his powers,
In their confluctions, all to run one way,
This may be truly said to be a Humour.
But that a rook, in wearing a pied feather,
The cable hat-band, or the three-piled riff,
A yard of shoe tie, or the Switzer's knot
On his French garters, should affect a Humour!
Oh, 'tis more than most ridiculous.

Cordatus replies:

He speaks pure truth now, if an Idiot
Have but an apish, or phantastic strain,
It is his Humour.

And Asper continues:

                    Well I will scourge these apes;
And to these courteous eyes oppose a mirror,
As large as is the stage, whereon we act:
Where they shall see the time's deformity
Anatomized in every nerve, and sinew,
With constant courage, and contempt of fear.

What was new in Jonson's approach, and what he began to initiate in the earlier *Every Man in His Humour*, is not, however, contained in this exposition. His didactic purpose was, like that of every true satirist, 'to scourge the follies of the time': broadly, to castigate the essential selfishness of individual affectations and pretensions on the grounds that it detracted from the serious and reasonable conduct of affairs. In his best plays, such as *Volpone*, he transcends this intention, and produces a subtle and poetic view of life that is quite beyond satire; nevertheless, his actual programme remained what one might call—in contrast to less self-consciously articulate dramatists such as Shakespeare or Webster or even Middleton—prosaic. What Jonson did above all, and he was more than fumbling towards it in *Every Man in His Humour*—was to bring home the vices and follies and 'humours' of people by presenting them in the familiar milieu of real life, as it might be projected on to the stage. In the original Quarto the play is set in Italy; it was clearly important to Jonson that he should transfer this to London. He himself saw more clearly that *Every Man in His Humour* had marked the beginning of 'his studies of this kind'. What concerned him was not the humour-theory itself, but the dramatic psychology which he had used this theory to implement. The theory in itself, after all, when divorced from the specific 'humour' terminology, is commonplace enough.

It seems likely that Jonson had written plays in collaboration with that other shamefully neglected Elizabethan Classicist, George Chapman. In May 1597 Henslowe presented a play by Chapman called *An Humourous Day's Mirth*, of which a Quarto text appeared in 1599. Thus Chapman precedes Jonson in his use of the 'humour' catchword in a play title. Furthermore, although his play is structurally a shambles in comparison to Jonson's, it bears many resemblances—some of them not superficial. Critics do not on the whole like Chapman (who did not much like them), and many have strenuously tried to deny that Jonson could have been at all influenced by him or by his play. Until towards the end of the last century it was even thought that *An Humourous Day's Mirth* was written after *Every Man in His Humour*. A reading of Chapman's play demonstrates that it must have suggested a great deal to Jonson. The type represented by Brainworm (Musco in the Quarto) is admittedly derived directly from the comedies of Plautus and Terence; but we see him first in his Elizabethan rôle as Lemot in *An Humourous Day's Mirth*: Lemot's part in this play is exactly the same as Brainworm's in *Every Man in His Humour*. He loves intrigue for its own sake, and his machinations are entirely responsible for the action. (I suggest that Chapman developed him from the central character of his first play, *The Blind Beggar of Alexandria*—of which only a mutilated text exists—whose quasi-Marlovian aspirations he seems entirely to drop.) Chapman's play is untidy, and his approach to his 'humourous' theme is more casual—it is even frivolous—and less methodical than Jonson's. But it would be unfair to underestimate

Chapman's general, as opposed to specific, influence on Jonson in this connection. Nor can the possibility be discounted that the two men discussed the question. Chapman wrote plays to earn a living, and must have taken at least his earlier dramatic writing less seriously than Jonson—who took everything he did seriously, thus incidentally elevating the status of printed plays from that enjoyed by newspaper cartoons today to the comparative dignity of the Shakespeare and Fletcher folios of a quarter of a century later. It is difficult to read *An Humourous Day's Mirth* and to discount the notion that the germ of *Every Man in His Humour* is there. But for Jonson's own achievement, apart from influences and theory, even in this early work, we have to look at the play itself.

THE PLAY

We need here to consider *Every Man in His Humour* in the revised Folio text: to give Jonson the benefit of his mature wisdom, and of his retrospectively clearer picture of his intentions. In the 1616 version he carefully presented the play as he wished it to be seen and read. We can be sure that he gave it very special attention, because he chose it to begin the Folio—ignoring *The Case is Altered* (published 1609), which is known to be earlier, altogether.

There is no known source for the play, and it is unlikely that one existed. However, considered solely in terms of dramatic structure, every element in it can be regarded as characteristically Latin. The plot is of the slightest: Old Kno'well intercepts a racy letter from young Wellbred to his son, Edward: full of kindly but misguided concern for his (and the whole younger generation's) welfare, he decides to spy on him. He unwisely confides in his servant, Brainworm, who decides not only to aid his young master in misleading his old, but also to enjoy himself thoroughly in a variety of comic disguises. Meanwhile, the merchant, Kitely, is suffering from violent jealousy as he imagines Wellbred (who lives in his home) and his 'loose' friends sexually enjoying his wife and his sister, Bridget. The two gulls Stephen and Matthew—both of whom *affect* humours, and are fit only for 'scourging' according to Jonson's later iteration of his principles—Bobadill, the boastful soldier, and Cob the water-carrier are incidental to the main action. In the end Clement, 'an old merry magistrate', 'purges' the main characters of their humours, i.e. 'cures' them, by making them see and realize their follies.

Situation in this play is a device, and so, really, is the whole theme of humours and their purgation. Our interest is not engaged by the stereotyped Terentian situation (the well-balanced, gay young men, the over-concerned father, the witty and resourceful servant, and environment of dupes and idiots, the sympathetic girl waiting to be rescued from the clutches of the old and dull) or by the theory; but

we are happy enough to countenance them as providing Jonson's
excuse to write a mainly lightweight but witty, neat and amusing
comedy about vanity and irrational impulses.

The best verse in *Every Man in His Humour* is spoken by Kitely.
He and Old Kno'well—and to a limited extent the angry Downright
—are the only real 'humour' characters in the play. Old Kno'well's
character suffers in interest because originally he had been basically
concerned about his son's defection to poetry; this had not been
fully exploited in Q, but had been rather abruptly and, dramatically,
ineffectively taken up after a lapse of four acts; with the poetry
theme removed, Old Kno'well becomes in F a faithfully-enough-
presented and convincing, but slightly stereotyped figure; his 'cure'
at the end is somewhat bathetic. His long soliloquy about the short-
comings of the younger generation, which begins II, iii, certainly
represents an acute observation of how the old do in fact think of
the young; but it can hardly be called original (it is in fact largely
based on passages from Quintilian and Juvenal), and he remains
dramatically uninteresting and lacking in potential.

Kitely is a different matter. This is a character-study that goes
beyond the scope of the merely comic or satirical. It is surely signi-
ficant that Garrick, in butchering the play, chose to build his
adaptation round the figure of Kitely. It is true that Kitely is very
funny, and that when he begins to think his clothes have been
poisoned he may seem to have become farcical; but in him Jonson
gives a realistic and subtle character-study of a compulsive neurotic.
It is wrong to take Kitely as merely the type of jealousy, or to
imagine that Jonson did not know (especially in the revision)
exactly what he was about. Kitely's insight into his own hopeless
condition is recognized and commented upon by editors and critics;
what is not noted is that there is no more precisely drawn character
in English drama (outside Shakespeare) before 1598. Marlowe never
tries to do this kind of thing, and one can search through the appren-
tice work of Dekker, and others who began writing for Henslowe
earlier than Jonson, in vain for anything approaching this exactitude
of character delineation; I have tried in my notes to indicate the
subtlety and depth of the portrait. Mr. Sale draws attention in his
edition to the dialect word 'kittle', meaning 'ticklish', i.e., 'hard to
deal with, touchy'; but he has missed the verb 'to kittle': 'to stir,
with feeling or emotion, usually pleasurable'. This, I think, together
with the obvious bird association, gives us a clue to Kitely's deepest
motives: his horror of becoming a cuckold is a rationalization of his
unconscious desire to be made into one—or rather, to see himself
being made into one. It was also clear to Jonson that Kitely perversely
enjoyed his wife less as a direct sexual object than as the indirect
object by which he might be cuckolded, 'wronged'. And by being
'wronged' Kitely could achieve two desires at once: he could gratify

his hidden voyeuristic impulse and purge his guilt about it by becoming a socially respectable 'victim'. His continual dread that 'it must be happening' is the result of his hidden wish to dwell on the details. Although he has to be 'cured' in 'the happy ending' demanded by the conventions of the audience-catching play Jonson was trying to write, his last remarks are, to say the least, ambiguous (V, i). The primarily sexual nature of his illness is perhaps hinted at in his 'horns' obsession: inevitably the cuckold's horns themselves are associated with the singular, sexually denotive, 'horn' (erect penis): thus in Kitely the voyeuristic origins of his state of mind are linguistically implied in the ostensibly 'justified' and 'reasonable' obsession. This is not, I believe, being over-subtle or reading into Jonson what is not there; one can grant him his share of the intuitions about modern psychological 'discoveries' that Freud himself allowed to poets and writers. The measure of his achievement is that the foundations are there upon which to deduce this—just as they might be in a real person.

T. S. Eliot said that Jonson created his own (aesthetic) world, and that nothing means anything outside this world; that his plays create themselves. Eliot was good at turning faintly ambiguous generalizations into particularizations that sound like critical master-strokes; this one is challenged early on in Jonson's career by his portraiture of Kitely: this character comes from life. His illness is funny—but Jonson does not achieve his comic effects by making him absurd; he simply continues to sketch in the portrait-from-life. He is funny because, as we know, life is funnier than anything we can make up about it.

The other characters do not rise to this superlative level of characterization, which foreshadows, in a developed and poetically enriched form, the triumphs of *Volpone*, *The Alchemist* and *Epicene*. Nevertheless, within their arbitrary framework, they provide Jonson with plenty of opportunity for valid ridicule and sharp characterization. The two young men, Edward Kno'well and Wellbred, are not intrinsically interesting: their function is vehicular, and they are merely 'flat' portraits of educated, well balanced and unaffected citizens. They do provide a contrast to the ill-balanced personalities of their elders, but there is very little attempt to make them characters in their own right. They are types, and their effectiveness on the stage must depend almost entirely upon the charm of the actors who play them.

Stephen, the town gull, and Matthew, the country gull and 'poet', are caricatures—but only just. They are nearer to reality than, I think, Jonson has been given credit for. Nor are they so entirely representative of the follies of only their own times as has been generally assumed. Such types are still with us—we only have to think, and we realize that we have met them, and dismissed them, perhaps, as being more fictional than real. There is room today for a Jonsonian satire on literary manners: on ignorance, vanity, pomposity, lack of humour, lack of talent. Probably there always has been and always will be. Realization of this fact helps us to see Jonson's intentions more clearly. There is at least a resemblance of attitude between Jonson's castigation of the poetasters of his time and Wyndham Lewis's of the poseurs of his: the man of genuine intellect and literary standards attacking the pretentious, the silly, the mere performer. What concerned Jonson was that people like Stephen and Matthew should ever be taken seriously as citizens; that is why their (and Bobadill's) punishment at the end of the play is so much more severe than anyone else's (in Q of course it was almost cruel, a detail that Jonson quite properly toned down): Matthew's 'poems' are burnt, and the two of them are excluded from the supper. This means that they are past 'cure'. Jonson believed that human nature could change, but not that fools could be turned into wise men.

Bobadill is a different matter, and his exile to the court at the end, 'to penitently fast it out', is even a matter for some regret; one feels that this fake's act is so colourful that for the sake of it he might have been let in on the supper. Like Kitely, but to a lesser extent, Bobadill is an intrinsically interesting character operating in isolation: the pseudo-Latin structure of the play itself will not let him develop. There is some dignity in him (where there is none at all in Stephen and Matthew), in his splendid correctness—even when exposed as a fake, a coward and not a true soldier—and some real pathos, which comes across strongly to reader and audience alike, in the very fact that while he can manage to be so magnificently correct in defeat, he cannot manage to be courageous, which is just the quality his act demands. He has antecedents as a rôle, but in presenting him as a type Jonson was original; and again, he is a good deal more credibly affecting than is often allowed. His 'We will have a bunch of radish, and salt, to taste our wine; and a pipe of tobacco, to close the orifice of the stomach' is more than an appealingly human touch: it sets the character before us, as a man, so that we interest ourselves in his fate. We can have no interest in what has no meaning 'outside itself'. It puts him outside the range of the author's own satiric purpose in respect of him. Perhaps Jonson realized this when he deliberately deleted a Q reference to him as a fellow gull of Matthew's. He has, in distinction to Matthew, some initiative: he arranges his life. Baskerville rightly found his prototype more in Crackstone of *Fedele and Fortunio* (*c.* 1584: a translation of Pasqualigo's *Il Fedele* perhaps by Stephen Gosson) and in Basilisco of Kyd's translation, *Soliman and Perseda*, rather than in the more familiar Plautine Miles Gloriosus rôle, the specifically boastful soldier. But in Bobadill we find something that is new: an imaginative vitality in fantasy for its own sake. His fantasy of himself and another selected nineteen's taking over the entire defence of the country—'provided, there be no treason practised upon us'—has a glorious life of its own: in some way the false act of the braggart half-redeems him, because it is natural to him, he feels it, he is utterly serious and correct about it, and wholly absorbed in it; in that way at least he lacks the essential frivolousness of Stephen and Matthew.

Cob is a mixture of individual, chorus (e.g. his comments on 'humour') and foil (his jealousy comically parodies Kitely's). He would have been a highly popular character with the audience in 1598, with his tirades against the hated fasting-days, and was no doubt skilfully and deliberately used by Jonson to appeal to the groundlings. There are hints of Jonson's later brilliance in the speeches he is given: as Jonas A. Barish has pointed out, in his opening monologue his is revealed as 'a mind myopically in pursuit of the object nearest it, unable to hold more than one thing at a time'; he sees through Matthew and even Bobadill, but cannot understand why he does so. This portrait, again, is drawn from life; seldom has plebeian near-illiteracy combined with native shrewdness been so cleverly and faithfully reproduced; yet still Jonson, because of a mischievous remark, is widely supposed to write plays that have no meaning 'outside themselves'.

The treatment of Downright, whose humour is of course anger, is perfunctory and the most academic in the play. The 'purging' of this humour is unconvincing, and it is likely that the audience might prefer to see him receive some rather more severe come-uppance. But the portrait itself, while a simple one, is successful, and gives the actor every chance to develop it. He also contrasts well with Kitely, in that he over-trusts appearances where the other over-fears them.

In terms of the play itself, Brainworm is not an exciting character; but the fact that he was almost certainly played by Burbage would have more than made up for this. (Edward Kno'well's exclamation 'An artificer! An architect! Except a man had studied begging all his lifetime, and been a weaver of language, from his infancy, for the clothing of it! I never saw his rival', III, ii, is almost certainly a personal tribute to Burbage.) In terms of the dramatic development, however, Brainworm is vital: he is the subversive hero, the honest and clever rogue, the type that absorbed Jonson throughout his life. His function is looked upon by many critics with some distaste—Mr. Sale's commentary on the play, for example, is peppered with derogatory remarks about him. But this disapproval—which has distorted almost all criticism of Jonson—is based on a superficial and conformist outlook with which he would have had no sympathy. Mr. Sale shows some awareness of this when he writes, though with more than a hint of disapproval, that Jonson 'is a thoroughly unorthodox moralist; it is the morality of the enemies, not of the pillars, of society. Brainworm is a faint dawning of this Villon strain. . . .'

Much stress is laid on Jonson's didactic purpose as a playwright, and perhaps rightly so. But a confusion creeps in, much akin to that made by the unenlightened who equate law or authority with moral goodness. Like his contemporary dramatists, Shakespeare included, Jonson was not an upholder of what in these days we call the Establishment. (To say that he or Shakespeare wanted to destroy the *status quo* would, of course, be wrong, too: the problem is more complicated than this.) But he had to be careful. He had taken it upon himself to raise the prestige of not only the poet but also the dramatist—on ostensibly Sidneyan lines, though an aristocrat like Sidney would never have approved of the vernacular mode or of the creation of an independent, published, active literature. In his self-conscious utterances about poetry, as in the Prologue to *Every Man in His Humour*, Jonson was almost exclusively Sidneyan and academic, realizing that only this kind of approach could meet with acceptance. But in his dramatic practice he was anything but academic; his subversive satire was more carefully worked out than that of any other writer of his time. Thus, Volpone's final words may indeed be justified as innocuous on the academic grounds that 'the play itself should please'; but they mean something quite different: 'I know we've had to have this "moral" ending, but you and I know differently'. A discussion of this problem as applied to Jonson's drama as a whole would be out of place here; but we get a strong foretaste of it in this play.

It is true that Clement, the 'purger of the humours', is somewhat of a stock figure, and that the ending in which he performs his function is a frankly contrived one. But even in these dramatically rather straitened circumstances Jonson manages to smuggle in an undeniably sharp piece of social satire. For Brainworm, the liar, the crook, is the magistrate's hero. In Q he was to be dressed in the magistrate's robes, and to preside; in F this is cut out. But Jonson's meaning is still clear. It is a topsy-turvy world. Authority itself is exactly what it ostensibly condemns. If there are true moral values, he is in effect, saying then these won't be found in those who publicly uphold them. This magistrate is—Brainworm! There is some implicit criticism, too, in the portrait of Clement when he first appears, before his function becomes wholly choric and purgative: hare-brained, sickeningly facetious, wholly personal in his inter-pretation of the law (as Wellbred says, III, ii, 260–1). Mr. Sale laments that his clerk, Formal, has an unfairly bad time—he is insulted, robbed, left naked in a tavern, and then excluded from the supper. But is this not because Jonson was fundamentally out of sympathy with such officious figures as magistrates' clerks—whether fairly or not?

As Helena Watts Baum has pointed out in her *Ben Jonson's Comedy*, Jonson's real didactic purpose was to show that poetry—as opposed to poetasting—was a serious and valuable activity. *Every Man in His Humour* is in one sense a weak play because neither in Q nor F does it really ever begin to show how poetry is in fact, or can be, a serious matter: Edward Kno'well is little more than a cipher, and one can draw no inferences from his speech or behaviour as to what virtue is like in action. This weakness led earlier critics such as Elizabeth Woodbridge to write: 'In *Every Man in His Humour* there are a number of rogues and a few honest men, but the line of division is drawn, not on a basis of honesty, but of wit. The three witty rogues . . . are successful in discomfiting not only the other rogues, but also the honest men. . . . Such a play can scarcely be called moral. . . . If it teaches anything, it teaches that it is convenient to have a quick brain, a ready tongue, and an elastic conscience'. This is not by any means poor criticism, for although it is wrong in relation to Jonson's intentions as we can tell them to have been by our study of his later work, it is nearly justified in respect of the play under discussion. The key phrase is 'the line of division is drawn . . . on a basis . . . of wit'. It is; and in this prentice play Jonson did not define clearly enough what he meant. Brainworm, for example, is only a cipher—largely owing to his having been conceived as a vehicle for Burbage, no doubt, who could be relied upon to add his own unique touches; he has nothing to say about why he acts as he does, and it is left to Clement at the end to 'recognize' him as the play's true hero.

Many people, including police officers, have a sympathy with confidence-men, because they know that these criminals imaginatively exploit the most vicious and acquisitive features of their 'marks' or victims. Jonson undoubtedly shared this sympathy, and the subtle, profound and dynamic development of this attitude in him is essential to our understanding of him; but the attitude is by no means as irresponsible or unserious as (for example) Mr. Sale hints. To think that it is is to pay mere lip service to Jonson. The artistic justification for Brainworm's conventionally improper triumph (apart from his little moment of discomfiture), which so upsets Mr. Sale, may not be fully apparent in the play in which he appears; it became so in *Volpone*.

To sum up, *Every Man in His Humour* is a play whose interest largely depends, for the audience, upon how it is acted, and for the reader, on its important position in Jonson's canon, as his first mature play. If Jonson had written nothing else, however, it would still be remembered for its unusually tight structure, for the at first nearly tragic and finally richly comic portrait of

Kitely, for Cob, Bobadill and for the so effectively lampooned gulls. If it is a modest play, it is so only in relation to the later work of its author.

Jonson's revision of Q bears all the marks of a supreme master of his craft. Here is an early play, which Jonson must have been sorely tempted to rewrite altogether (as he probably did *A Tale of a Tub* when he was an old man); instead of this he wisely left it alone, merely toning down excesses and imbalances of plot, brilliantly transferring it to the London of 1598, in which he had really first conceived it and, finally, bringing the manner of the dialogue up to date and generally sharpening it up. Of all the known revisions in English literature, this, though modest, is the most impressive—indeed, its modesty is one of its most telling features; had Jonson tried to do more to the play, he must have succeeded only in destroying it.

A full account of the revision is given in H. H. Carter's useful annotated edition of 1921, which prints the Quarto and Folio texts in parallel. What follows here is a brief summary of the changes Jonson made, with a fuller note of some of the more important ones.

1. The scene is changed from Florence to London, in accordance with Jonson's assertion in the prologue to *The Alchemist* that 'Our scene is London, 'cause we would make known/No country's mirth is better than our own'. The improvement is undoubted, and is confined to names of places: vague references are particularized, and the whole action gains in realism. The names of the characters are of course changed, to some advantage: Lorenzo Senior and Junior become Kno'well and Edward Kno'well; Prospero becomes Wellbred; Hesperida becomes Bridget; Stepheno, Matheo and Bobadillo are anglicized; Thorello becomes Kitely; Musco becomes Brainworm, Piza, Cash, and Giulliano Downright.

2. There is a good deal of condensation. We can include under this heading both cuts in the length of speeches and the introduction of contracted forms—'have' to 'ha' ', 'in' to 'i' ', 'of' to 'o' ' and 'and' to 'an' '. A representative list of these may be found in Carter.

3. The structural alterations improve the play without changing it. Seeing that the poetry-theme was not properly followed through, and realizing that it could not be without serious damage to the play, Jonson made it merely incidental. He made Clement reprimand Kno'well for his general dislike of poetry, and simultaneously voice Jonson's own all-important distinction between true and false poets; but he completely—and, in the play's interest, rightly—cut Lorenzo Junior's famous defence of poetry. His father says to him:

                         . . . you see
How abjectly your Poetry is ranked,
In general opinion.

And he replies:

Opinion, Oh God let gross opinion
Sink and be damned as deep as Barathrum.
If it may stand with your most wished content,
I can refell opinion, and approve
The state of poesy, such as it is,
Blessed, eternal, and most true divine:
Indeed if you will look on Poesy,
As she appears in many, poor and lame,
Patched up in remnants and old worn rags,
Half-starved for want of her peculiar food,
Sacred invention, then I must confirm,
Both your conceit and censure of her merit.
But view her in her glorious ornaments,
Attired in the majesty of art,
Set high in spirit with the precious taste
Of sweet philosophy, and which is most,
Crowned with the rich traditions of a soul
That hates to have her dignity profaned,
With any relish of an earthly thought:
Oh then how proud a presence doth she bear.
Then is she like her self, fit to be seen
Of none but grave and consecrated eyes:
Nor is it any blemish to her fame,
That such lean, ignorant, and blasted wits,
Such brainless gulls, should utter their stol'n wares
With such applauses in our vulgar ears:
Or that their slubbered lines have current pass,
From the fat judgements of the multitudes,
But that this barren and infected age,
Should set no differences twixt these empty spirits,
And a true Poet: than which reverend name,
Nothing can more adorn humanity.

Other scenes and passages were cut: Clement's visit to Kitely's
house and a superfluous explanation by Brainworm of his machinations. Clement's admiration of Brainworm and the punishment of
Matthew and Bobadill were both toned down: in the Quarto
Brainworm was to preside over the table in the Justice's robes, and
Matthew and Bobadill were to spend the night in a cage as a prelude
to the pillory, in which they were to sing a penitential ballad to the
tune of 'Who list to lead a soldier's life'. The Justice's admiration of
Brainworm is an essential feature of the play; but perhaps Jonson
realized that in later plays he had made this point about authority
more clearly, and so softened it in F.

4. Just as he condensed some passages, so Jonson expanded others, almost always enriching them. Again, Carter prints a representative list of these expansions.

5. There is a general tightening up of language. Just as the setting is transformed from a vague Florence to a precise and lifelike London, so the language is given new life, vigour and directness. 'At study' becomes 'at his book', 'ere it be long' 'again' winter', and so on: the effect is cumulative.

6. Although the introduction to a modernized edition is no place to discuss them, the various syntactical changes made by Jonson should be made the subject of a special study: they are of the utmost importance both as examples of Jonson's own changed practice and the rapid and not yet fully charted changes in the English language that took place in his time. Carter's notes treat some of these in detail, but the time is now ripe, as Mr. A. C. Partridge has suggested in *Orthography and Elizabethan Drama* (1964), for a comprehensive study of them.

7. *The Prologue*—which might in a sense be said to replace Lorenzo Junior's cut defence of poetry—is added for the first time in F. It is an 'official' piece, based almost exclusively on Sidneyan principles; but it was important to Jonson because in effect it prefaced his entire folio collection—the first book ever to regard plays as serious works, to be counted in with poems.

8. Oaths are an important feature of both Q and F; but the 1605/6 Act restraining the use of oaths by players forced him to soften those of Q. He performed this softening with his tongue in his cheek, and it is quite obvious that he had the same kind of contempt for this Act that we nowadays reserve for censorship boards or watch-committees. Direct references to God are avoided in almost one hundred instances, so that 'by God' becomes 'by my fackins', 'by God's will', 'by Gad's lid', and so on. The shift is that familiar hypocritical one from directness to permitted euphemism, and Jonson was quite aware of this. His own attitude may well be indicated in a change he made in III, iii, when Cob is suing for his warrant against Downright. In both texts, Clement reprimands Cob when he begs 'Oh, I beseech your worship, for God's sake, dear Master Justice' by answering 'Nay, God's precious . . .', i.e. don't swear by God. In Q, in his later expostulatory speech beginning 'What? a threadbare rascal . . .', he exclaims 'by God's passion'; in F this is ironically cut to 'by God's precious—I say, go to' where the dash evidently represents some other 'offensive' word which Clement (the magistrate) does not utter only because he has just reprimanded Cob. But while Jonson is critical of the official attitude toward oaths in F, he retains and even amplifies his satire on their use by Stephen's weak imitations of Bobadill's perfection in the art.

9. The characterization of F is markedly superior to that of Q.

The thesis that Jonson decided 'to integrate the humour business with the action and the structure of the play', advanced in J. A. Bryant's article in *Studies in Philology* (LIX, 1962) is somewhat fanciful, I feel, as is the notion that 'Acts I and II present the accumulation of symptoms, Act III the aggravation, Act IV the crisis, and Act V the cure'; Jonson in his revision does not succeed in turning the play into 'his first and only fully realized humour play' in anything but a wholly academic and strained sense. But Old Kno'well does become a more credible figure when the poetry-theme is softened, and he is thus turned into a more conventionally worried father, and Bobadill's bragging does become more fantastic-ally pointless, and the language of Kitely's jealous mind is given, at points, a greater edge and precision. The improvements are nearly all ones of detail; they do not make the play into something it was not before, but help to perfect the small but fine thing that it always was.

NOTE ON THE TEXT

THIS TEXT IS based upon the 1616 Folio, and follows it very closely in everything but spelling, which has been regularized and modernized. This differs from other modern editions in following Jonson's punctuation, on the grounds that he himself undoubtedly saw it through the press, and was seriously concerned with this aspect of the text. His own punctuation, though very heavy by modern standards, still remains by far the best guide to the delivery of his lines; in reading through a standard re-punctuated text such as Mr. Sale's or Schelling's 1910 edition, one continually feels the loss: the superimposition of modern punctuation techniques, which are wholly logical, is simply not an effective substitute; the rhythm is continually ruined, the sense—or at any rate the emphases— sometimes slightly distorted.

However, certain changes have been made, usually silently, to bring the text into line with what are felt to be the reasonable requirements of a modern reader:

1. Jonson used brackets, not always consistently, to indicate a number of things, such as asides, and exclamations: these have been removed and commas, exclamations or stage directions (usually 'aside') have been substituted.

2. Not all Jonson's italics and initial capitals have been retained, but only those that now seem to have some special significance.

3. Jonson's own stage directions have been retained—whenever they occur in the middle of a speech his marginal directions are placed in round brackets—but these have been amplified, although minimally; all editorial additions are in square brackets. F heads each scene with the names of all the characters that appear in it, regardless of whether they enter at the beginning of the scene or not; such characters in these 'block entries' as do not enter at the beginning of the scene are omitted, but are not introduced in square brackets when they do enter because they have appeared in F at the head of the scene. My stage-directions are based on Nicholson's old Mermaid edition, which were in turn based on—but improved— Gifford's; I do not often deviate from these.

4. Gifford's scene-divisions have been adopted, in line with modern practice; but Jonson's own F divisions, which are formal rather than practical, have been noted.

5. The obvious corrections that the printers of the 1640 Folio made in the text have been silently adopted; in most instances, though not in all, I have followed Herford and Simpson; I have occasionally made a correction where they have retained the 1616 reading on the grounds

that it represented possible practice at the time of publication. Where emendations give rise to doubt or interest, which in this text is seldom, they have been noted.

6. 'O', 'Oh', 'o', spelt thus variously by Jonson, has been regularized to 'Oh'.

7. The contraction 'Mr.' has been expanded to 'Master'.

8. 'God' has been given an initial capital in deference to modern convention and usage.

9. Elisions of verbal endings in 'ed' have not been retained. Where the text does not elide it is assumed that the reader will know when to sound the last vowel.

FURTHER READING

Barish, J. A. *Jonson and the Language of Prose Comedy*. New York, 1960.

Baskerville, C. R. *English Elements in Jonson's Early Comedy*. Texas, 1911.

Baum, H. W. *The Satiric and the Didactic in Jonson's Comedy*. Chapel Hill, 1947.

Bryant, J. A. 'Jonson's Revision of Every Man in His Humour', *Studies in Philology*, LIX, 1962.

Carter, H. H. (ed.). Facsimile Reprint of Quarto and Folio texts of *Every Man in His Humour*. New Haven, 1921.

Ellis-Fermor, U. *The Jacobean Drama* (chapter on Jonson). London, 1936 and 1965.

Enck, J. J. *Jonson and the Comic Truth*. Madison, 1957.

Herford, C. H. and Simpson, P. *Ben Jonson*. 11 vols. Oxford, 1925–52.

Knights, L. C. *Drama and Society in the Age of Jonson*. London, 1937.

Sackton, A. H. *Rhetoric as a Dramatic Language in Jonson*. New York, 1948.

Townsend, F. L. *Apologie for Bartholomew Fayre: The Art of Jonson's Comedies*. New York, 1947.

For other useful editions of *Every Man in His Humour* see *Acknowledgements*.

There is no wholly satisfactory biography of Jonson. The best, albeit somewhat dry and fragmentary, is in Herford and Simpson. *Ben Jonson of Westminster* by Marchette Chute (London, 1954) may be read, but with a very critical eye. For later biographical research see articles cited in *Cambridge Bibliography of English Literature*, Vol. 1, 1940, and *Supplement*, 1957.

Euery
MAN IN
HIS
HVMOVR.

A Comœdie.

Acted in the yeere 1598. By the then
Lord Chamberlaine his
Seruants.

The Author B. I.

IUVEN.

Haud tamen inuideas vati, quem pulpita pafcunt.

LONDON,
Printed by WILLIAM STANSBY.

M. DC. XVI.

'TO THE MOST LEARNED, AND MY HONOURED FRIEND
Master Camden, CLARENCEUX.

SIR, There are, no doubt, a supercilious race in the world,
who will esteem all office, done you in this kind, an injury; so
solemn a vice it is with them to use the authority of their   5
ignorance, to the crying down of Poetry, or the Professors:
but, my gratitude must not leave to correct their error; since
I am none of those, that can suffer the benefits conferred upon
my youth, to perish with my age. It is a frail memory, that
remembers but present things: and, had the favour of the   10
times so conspired with my disposition, as it could have
brought forth other, or better, you had had the same proportion, and number of the fruits, the first. Now, I pray you, to
accept this, such, wherein neither the confession of my
manners shall make you blush; nor of my studies, repent you   15
to have been the instructor: and, for the profession of my
thankfulness, I am sure, it will, with good men, find either
praise, or excuse.

                          Your true lover,
                             BEN. JONSON.

---

7 *leave* omit

---

2 William Camden (1551–1623), the antiquary, was Jonson's schoolmaster
  at Westminster. See *Epigrams*, XIV. Camden was made Clarenceux, the
  second of the three English Kings-of-Arms, in 1597.

The Persons of the Play.

KNO'WELL, an old gentleman.
ED. KNO'WELL, his son.
BRAINWORM, the father's man.
Master STEPHEN, a country gull.
[GEORGE] DOWNRIGHT, a plain squire.   5
WELLBRED, his half-brother.
Justice CLEMENT, an old merry magistrate.
ROGER FORMAL, his clerk.
[THOMAS] KITELY, a merchant.
Dame KITELY, his wife.   10
Mistress BRIDGET, his sister.
Master MATTHEW, the town gull.
[THOMAS] CASH, Kitely's man.
[OLIVER] COB, a water-bearer.
TIB, his wife.   15
Captain BOBADILL, a Paul's man.
[SERVANTS, etc.]

The Scene.
LONDON.

4, 12 *gull* dupe

14 *water-bearer.* In Jonson's time water had to be fetched from the con-
   duits. Water-bearers were sometimes called cobs.
16 *Bobadill.* Boabdill, a corruption of Abu'Abd Allah, was the last king of
   the Moors in Spain (1492).
   Paul's man. A fashionable man-about-town; specifically, a frequenter
   of the middle aisle of St. Paul's, then both a centre of business and a
   place . . . in which 'to be seen'.

EVERY MAN IN HIS HUMOUR

Prologue

Though need make many Poets, and some such
As art, and nature have not bettered much;
Yet ours, for want, hath not so loved the stage,
As he dare serve th'ill customs of the age:
Or purchase your delight at such a rate,   5
As, for it, he himself must justly hate.
To make a child, now swaddled, to proceed
Man, and then shoot up, in one beard, and weed,
Past threescore years: or, with three rusty swords,
And help of some few foot-and-half-foot words,   10
Fight over York, and Lancaster's long jars:
And in the tiring-house bring wounds, to scars.
He rather prays, you will be pleased to see
One such, to-day, as other plays should be.
Where neither Chorus wafts you o'er the seas;   15
Nor creaking throne comes down, the boys to please;
Nor nimble squib is seen, to make afeared
The gentlewomen; nor rolled bullet heard
To say, it thunders; nor tempestuous drum
Rumbles, to tell you when the storm doth come;   20
But deeds, and language, such as men do use:
And persons, such as Comedy would choose,
When she would show an Image of the times,
And sport with human follies, not with crimes.
Except, we make 'hem such by loving still   25
Our popular errors, when we know they're ill.

12 *tiring-house* theatre dressing-room

---

10 *Foot-and-half-foot words*. In his translation of Horace's *De Arte Poetica*
   Jonson renders 'sesquipedalia verba' (l. 97), literally 'high-sounding
   words', by 'foot-and-half-foot words'.
11 i.e. Shakespeare's cycle of history plays, among others.
18–19 *nor . . . thunders*. Thunder was simulated by rolling a cannon-ball
   along the floor; the critic John Dennis (1657–1734) invented the
   modern method.
24 See Aristotle, *Poetics*, V, I, where he assigns the ridiculous as a fit
   subject for comedy, and the crimes of men to tragedy.
25 *'hem*. A form directly derived from Old English, not a contraction of
   'them' at all, although 'them' or ''em' eventually took its place.

7

I mean such errors, as you'll all confess
By laughing at them, they deserve no less:
Which when you heartily do, there's hope left, then,
You, that have so graced monsters, may like men.   30

Act I, Scene i

[*A Plot before* KNO'WELL'S *House*]

[*Enter*] KNO'WELL

KNO'WELL
A goodly day toward! And a fresh morning!
                                        Brainworm!

[*Enter*] BRAINWORM.

Call up your young master: bid him rise, sir.
Tell him, I have some business to employ him.
BRAINWORM
I will sir, presently.
KNO'WELL   But hear you, sirrah,
If he be' at his book, disturb him not.
BRAINWORM   Well sir.   5

[*Exit* BRAINWORM]

KNO'WELL
How happy, yet, should I esteem myself
Could I, by any practice, wean the boy
From one vain course of study, he affects.
He is a scholar, if a man may trust
The liberal voice of fame, in her report   10
Of good account, in both our universities,
Either of which hath favoured him with graces:
But their indulgence, must not spring in me
A fond opinion, that he cannot err.
Myself was once a student; and, indeed,   15
Fed with the self-same humour, he is now,

1 *toward* impending
4 *presently* immediately
5 *be'at* the apostrophe is metrical
  Well sir 'Very good, sir', Q, G, Sh
12 *graces* degrees

15–20 *Myself . . . knowledge.* These lines are adapted from Kyd's *The Spanish Tragedy*, VI.i, 71–74:

> When I was young I gave my mind
> And plied myself to fruitless poetry:
> Which though it profit the professor naught,
> Yet is it passing pleasing to the world.

Dreaming on nought but idle poetry,
That fruitless, and unprofitable art,
Good unto none, but least to the professors,
Which, then, I thought the mistress of all knowledge: 20
But since, time, and the truth have waked my judgement,
And reason taught me better to distinguish,
The vain, from th' useful learnings.

[*Enter*] MASTER STEPHEN

Cousin Stephen!
What news with you, that you are here so early?
STEPHEN
Nothing, but e'en come to see how you do, uncle.   25
KNO'WELL
That's kindly done, you are welcome, coz.
STEPHEN
Ay, I know that sir, I would not ha' come else. How do my
cousin Edward, uncle?
KNO'WELL
Oh, well coz, go in and see: I doubt he be scarce stirring yet.
STEPHEN
Uncle, afore I go in, can you tell me, an' he have e'er a book   30
of the sciences of hawking, and hunting? I would fain
borrow it.
KNO'WELL
Why, I hope you will not a hawking now, will you?
STEPHEN
No wusse; but I'll practise against next year uncle: I have
bought me a hawk, and a hood, and bells, and all; I lack   35
nothing but a book to keep it by.

19 *professors* those who practise it seriously
25 *e'en* only
30 *an'* both 'an' or 'and' (=an') could mean 'if'
31 *fain* gladly; eagerly
34 *wusse* certainly
    against in preparation for
36 *keep* observe (the art of hawking)

27 *do.* F2 corrects this vulgarism, but as Herford and Simpson point out, it
    suits Stephen, and is obviously intentional.
30–31 *book . . . hunting.* There were many such books. The most famous was
    The Gentleman's Academie (1486), reissued in 1595 by Gervase
    Markham. The full title of another work, by William Gryndall, pub-
    lished in 1596, gives a clue to the kind of gentlemanly status Stephen was
    seeking: *Hawking, Hunting, Fowling, and Fishing, . . . Whereunto is
    annexed, the manner and order in keeping of Hawks, their diseases, and
    cures: and all such special points, as any wise, appertain to so Gentleman-
    like quality.*

KNO'WELL

Oh, most ridiculous.

STEPHEN

Nay, look you now, you are angry, uncle: why you know,
an' a man have not skill in the hawking, and hunting-
languages nowadays, I'll not give a rush for him. They are   40
more studied than the Greek, or the Latin. He is for no
gallants' company without 'hem. And by gad's lid I scorn
it, I, so I do, to be a consort for every humdrum, hang 'hem
scroyles, there's nothing in 'hem, i' the world. What do you
talk on it? Because I dwell at Hogsden, I shall keep company   45
with none but the archers of Finsbury? Or the citizens, that
come a ducking to Islington ponds? A fine jest i' faith!
'Slid a gentleman mun show himself like a gentleman. Uncle,
I pray you be not angry, I know what I have to do, I trow,
I am no novice.   50

KNO'WELL

You are a prodigal absurd coxcomb: go to.
Nay never look at me, it's I that speak.
Take't as you will sir, I'll not flatter you.
Ha' you not yet found means enow, to waste
That, which your friends have left you, but you must   55
Go cast away your money on a kite,
And know not how to keep it, when you ha' done?
Oh it's comely! This will make you a gentleman!
Well cousin, well! I see you are e'en past hope
Of all reclaim. Ay, so, now you are told on it,   60
You look another way.

STEPHEN   What would you ha' me do?

KNO'WELL

What would I have you do? I'll tell you kinsman,
Learn to be wise, and practise how to thrive,
That would I have you do: and not to spend
Your coin on every bauble, that you fancy,   65

43 *humdrum* commonplace fellow
44 *scroyles* scoundrels
44–45 *What . . . it?* 'D'you mean to tell me that . . .'
45 *Hogsden* Hoxton, then one street among fields
47 *ducking* duck hunting with dogs
48 *'Slid* abbreviation of 'God's lid'
   mun must
49 *trow* trust
56 *kite* falcon

46 *the archers of Finsbury.* Finsbury fields had been made into an archery
   ground in 1498. In Jonson's time the lower classes frequented it: hence
   Stephen's indignation.

Or every foolish brain, that humours you.
I would not have you to invade each place,
Nor thrust yourself on all societies,
Till men's affections, or your own desert,
Should worthily invite you to your rank. 70
He, that is so respectless in his courses,
Oft sells his reputation, at cheap market.
Nor would I, you should melt away yourself
In flashing bravery, lest while you affect
To make a blaze of gentry to the world, 75
A little puff of scorn extinguish it,
And you be left, like an unsavoury snuff,
Whose property is only to offend.
I'd ha' you sober, and contain yourself;
Not, that your sail be bigger than your boat: 80
But moderate your expenses now, at first,
As you may keep the same proportion still.
Nor, stand so much on your gentility,
Which is an airy, and mere borrowed thing,
From dead men's dust, and bones: and none of yours 85
Except you make, or hold it. Who comes here?

[Enter a] SERVANT

SERVANT
Save you, gentlemen.
STEPHEN
Nay, we do' not stand much on our gentility, friend; yet,
you are welcome, and I assure you, mine uncle here is a man
of a thousand a year, Middlesex land: he has but one son in 90
all the world, I am his next heir, at the common law, Master
Stephen, as simple as I stand here, if my cousin die—as
there's hope he will—I have a pretty living o' my own too,
beside, hard by here.
SERVANT
In good time, sir. 95

71 *respectless* inconsiderate
74 *flashing bravery* gaudy, showy clothes
77 *unsavoury snuff* the stink of an extinguished candle
84 *airy* aërie, F1
87 begins Scene ii in Ff
   Save you 'God save you'
88 *do'not* the apostrophe indicates the pronunciation 'don't'

95 *In . . . sir.* A form of polite acquiescence, which Stephen deliberately
   misinterprets. However, Herford and Simpson point out that it could
   be ironic.

STEPHEN

   In good time, sir? Why! And in very good time, sir. You do
not flout, friend, do you?

SERVANT

   Not I, sir.

STEPHEN

   Not you, sir? You were not best, sir; an' you should, here
be them can perceive it, and that quickly too: go to. And they   100
can give it again soundly too, and need be.

SERVANT

   Why, sir, let this satisfy you: good faith, I had no such
intent.

STEPHEN

   Sir, an' I thought you had, I would talk with you, and that
presently.   105

SERVANT

   Good Master Stephen, so you may, sir, at your pleasure.

STEPHEN

   And so I would sir, good my saucy companion! An' you were
not o' mine uncle's ground, I can tell you; though I do not
stand upon my gentility neither in't.

KNO'WELL

   Cousin! cousin! Will this ne'er be left?   110

STEPHEN

   Whoreson base fellow! A mechanical serving-man! By this
cudgel, and't were not for shame, I would—

KNO'WELL

   What would you do, you peremptory gull?
If you cannot be quiet, get you hence.
You see, the honest man demeans himself   115
Modestly to'ards you, giving no reply
To your unseasoned, quarrelling, rude fashion:
And, still you huff it, with a kind of carriage,
As void of wit, as of humanity.
Go, get you in; fore heaven, I am ashamed   120
Thou hast a kinsman's interest in me.   [*Exit* STEPHEN]

SERVANT

   I pray you, sir. Is this Master Kno'well's house?

  97 *flout* mock
101 *and* if
105 *presently* immediately
111 *mechanical* base
113 *peremptory* utter
     gull credulous simpleton
117 *unseasoned* uncalled for; perhaps also meaning 'green'
118 *huff it* swagger

KNO'WELL

  Yes, marry, it is sir.

SERVANT

  I should enquire for a gentleman, here, one Master Edward
  Kno'well: do you know any such, sir, I pray you? 125

KNO'WELL

  I should forget myself else, sir.

SERVANT

  Are you the gentleman? Cry you mercy sir: I was required by
  a gentleman i' the city, as I rode out at this end o' the town,
  to deliver you this letter, sir.

KNO'WELL

  To me, sir! What do you mean? Pray you remember your 130
  court'sy. [*Reads*] 'To his most selected friend, Master
  Edward Kno'well.' What might the gentleman's name be,
  sir. that sent it? Nay, pray you be covered.

SERVANT

  One Master Wellbred, sir.

KNO'WELL

  Master Wellbred! A young gentleman? Is he not? 135

SERVANT

  The same sir, Master Kitely married his sister: the rich
  merchant i' the Old Jewry.

KNO'WELL

  You say very true. Brainworm!

               [*Enter*] BRAINWORM

BRAINWORM

  Sir.

KNO'WELL

  Make this honest friend drink here: pray you go in. 140

             [*Exeunt* BRAINWORM *and* SERVANT]

  This letter is directed to my son:
  Yet, I am Edward Kno'well too, and may
  With the safe conscience of good manners, use
  The fellow's error to my satisfaction.
  Well, I will break it ope—old men are curious— 145
  Be it but for the style's sake, and the phrase,
  To see, if both do answer my son's praises,
  Who is, almost, grown the idolater

---

123 *marry* oath: by Mary
130–131 *pray . . . court'sy* 'put on your hat' (i.e. 'you need not keep
    it off any longer')

---

137 *Old Jewry*. A street running off Poultry, near the modern Bank under-
    ground station.

Of this young Wellbred: what have we here? What's this?
([*Reads*] *the letter*) 'Why, Ned, I beseech thee; has thou   150
forsworn all thy friends i' the Old Jewry? Or dost thou think
us all Jews that inhabit there, yet? If thou dost, come over,
and but see our frippery: change an old shirt, for a whole
smock, with us. Do not conceive that antipathy between us,
and Hogsden; as was between Jews and hogs-flesh. Leave   155
thy vigilant father, alone, to number over his green apricots,
evening, and morning, o' the north-west wall: an' I had been
his son, I had saved him the labour, long since; if, taking in
all the young wenches, that pass by, at the back-door, and
coddling every kernel of the fruit for 'hem, would ha' served.   160
But, pr'ythee, come over to me, quickly, this morning: I
have such a present for thee (our Turkey company never
sent the like to the Grand Signior). One is a rhymer sir, o'
your own batch, your own leaven; but doth think himself
Poet-major, o' the town: willing to be shown, and worthy   165
to be seen. The other—I will not venture his description
with you, till you come, because I would ha' you make
hither with an appetite. If the worst of 'hem be not worth
your journey, draw your bill of charges, as unconscionable,
as any Guildhall verdict will give it you, and you shall be   170
allowed your viaticum.

153 *frippery* second-hand clothes' shop
158 *labour* this pun anticipates the one on 'coddling', 160 below
163 *Grand Signior* Sultan of Turkey
164 *batch* number of loaves baked at once; the metaphor is continued
       in *leaven* dough
171 *viaticum* expenses of the journey

151–152 *Or . . . yet.* The name Old Jewry was, of course, only a survival in
       Jonson's time.
153–154 *change . . . us.* 'Exchange a woman ("smock", used allusively) with-
       out venereal disease ("whole") for your testy old father ("old shirt").'
160 *coddling.* Stewing, but with plays on 'cods' (=scrotum, testicles) and
       'cuddling'; there could be a pun involved in 'taking in', but the first
       printed appearance of this in the sense of 'deceive' seems to be 1725.
162 *Turkey company.* Founded in 1579, and received its charter in 1581 for
       trade with the Levant. The costly presents sent to the Sultan to gain
       special trading privileges for the English were evidently a common
       subject of discussion.
165 *Poet-major, o' the town.* Evidently a retrospective hit at Anthony
       Munday (1554–1633); Q read, more topically, 'the Hall Beadle, or Poet
       Nuntius', although the whole passage is drastically rearranged.
169–170 *unconscionable . . . verdict.* The savagery of the sentences at Guild-
       hall was well-known. London and Middlesex juries in general were the
       object of popular dislike for their unfair severity.

                         From the Windmill.'
From the Bordello, it might come as well;
The Spittle: or Pict-hatch. Is this the man,
My son hath sung so, for the happiest wit,   175
The choicest brain, the times hath sent us forth?
I know not what he may be, in the arts;
Nor what in schools: but surely, for his manners,
I judge him a profane, and dissolute wretch:
Worse, by possession of such great good gifts,   180
Being the master of so loose a spirit.
Why, what unhallowed ruffian would have writ,
In such a scurrilous manner, to a friend!
Why should he think, I tell my Apricots?
Or play th' Hesperian Dragon, with my fruit,   185
To watch it? Well, my son, I' had thought
You'd had more judgement, t'have made election
Of your companions, than t'have ta'en on trust,
Such petulant, jeering gamesters, that can spare
No argument, or subject from their jest.   190
But I perceive, affection makes a fool
Of any man, too much the father. Brainworm!

                    [*Enter*] BRAINWORM

BRAINWORM
  Sir.
KNO'WELL
  Is the fellow gone that brought this letter?
BRAINWORM
  Yes, sir, a pretty while since.   195
KNO'WELL
  And, where's your young master?
BRAINWORM
  In his chamber sir.
KNO'WELL
  He spake not with the fellow! Did he?
BRAINWORM
  No sir, he saw him not.

173 *Bordello* brothel   184 *tell* count
186–187 *I'had thought/ You'd had* I'had thought/Y'had had, F1 I had
        thought you/Had had, G   189 *gamesters* jokers
_____

172 *the Windmill*. Originally a synagogue; by Jonson's time it had become a
    tavern.
174 *the Spittle*. Lazar-house; the reference here is to the *lock*, a hospital for
    venereal diseases at Kingsland near Hogsden.
    Pict-hatch a well-known prostitutes' beat near Clerkenwell Green.
185 *th' Hesperian Dragon*. Ladon, who assisted the Hesperides to guard over
    Hera's golden apples.

KNO'WELL

Take you this letter, and deliver it my son, but with no   200
notice, that I have opened it, on your life.

BRAINWORM

Oh lord, sir, that were a jest, indeed!   [*Exit* BRAINWORM]

KNO'WELL

I am resolved, I will not stop his journey;
Nor practise any violent mean, to stay
The unbridled course of youth in him: for that,   205
Restrained, grows more impatient; and, in kind,
Like to the eager, but the generous greyhound,
Who ne'er so little from his game withheld,
Turns head, and leaps up at his holder's throat.
There is a way of winning, more by love,   210
And urging of the modesty, than fear:
Force works on servile natures, not the free.
He, that's compelled to goodness, may be good;
But 'tis but for that fit: where others drawn
By softness, and example, get a habit.
Then, if they stray, but warn 'hem: and, the same
They should for virtue' have done, they'll do for shame.   215

                                                 [*Exit*]

Act I, Scene [ii]

[*A Room in* KNO'WELL'S *House*]

[*Enter*] ED. KNO'WELL, BRAINWORM

ED. KNO'WELL

Did he open it, sayest thou?

BRAINWORM

Yes, o' my word sir, and read the contents.

ED. KNO'WELL

That scarce contents me. What countenance, pr'ythee, made
he, i' the reading of it? Was he angy, or pleased?

BRAINWORM

Nay sir, I saw him not read it, nor open it, I assure your   5
worship.

200–201 *Take . . . life* printed as verse in F1
211 *modesty* self-control
      Scene [*ii*] Scene iii in Ff, but misnumbered ii therein

---

207 *generous.* High-spirited; well bred. But Jonson extends the meaning of
     this word to 'over-spirited': this is made clear by his use of the preced-
     ing 'but' and by ll. 208–209, 'Who . . . throat'.
210–214 These lines are adapted (and much improved) from Terence's
     Adelphi.

ED. KNO'WELL

No? How know'st thou, then, that he did either?

BRAINWORM

Marry sir, because he charged me, on my life, to tell nobody,
that he opened it: which, unless he had done, he would
never fear to have it revealed.   10

ED. KNO'WELL

That's true: well I thank thee, Brainworm.

[Moves to window to read letter]

[Enter] MASTER STEPHEN

STEPHEN

Oh, Brainworm, did'st thou not see a fellow here in a what-
sha'-call-him doublet? He brought mine uncle a letter e'en
now.

BRAINWORM

Yes, Master Stephen, what of him?   15

STEPHEN

Oh, I ha' such a mind to beat him—Where is he? Canst thou
tell?

BRAINWORM

Faith, he is not of that mind: he is gone, Master Stephen.

STEPHEN

Gone? Which way? When went he? How long since?

BRAINWORM

He is rid hence. He took horse, at the street door.   20

STEPHEN

And, I stayed i' the fields! Whoreson scanderbag rogue! Oh
that I had a horse to fetch him back again.

BRAINWORM

Why, you may ha' my master's gelding, to save your
longing, sir.

STEPHEN

But I ha' no boots, that's the spite on't.   25

BRAINWORM

Why, a fine wisp of hay, rolled hard, Master Stephen.

13 *doublet?; doublet!'*, F1

---

21 *scanderbag.* George Castriot (1414–1467), who won the freedom of his
native Albania from the Turks in a series of battles, was called by the
Turks Scanderbag (i.e., Iskander-bey: Prince Alexander). His life had
been translated by I. Gentleman (1596) and he is often alluded to,
notably by Dekker and by Gabriel Harvey in his extravagant, misin-
formed and pretentious stanzas on Marlowe's death.

26 *a fine wisp of hay, rolled hard.* A rustic practice, alluded to by Jonson in
A Tale of A Tub.

STEPHEN

No faith, it's no boot to follow him, now: let him e'en go, and hang. 'Pray thee, help to truss me, a little. He does so vex me—

BRAINWORM

You'll be worse vexed, when you are trussed, Master 30
Stephen. Best, keep unbraced; and walk yourself, till you be cold: your choler may founder you else.

STEPHEN

By my faith, and so I will, now thou tell'st me on't: how dost thou like my leg, Brainworm?

BRAINWORM

A very good leg, Master Stephen! But the woollen stocking 35
does not commend it so well.

STEPHEN

Foh, the stockings be good enough, now summer is coming on, for the dust: I'll have a pair of silk again winter, that I go to dwell i' the town. I think my leg would show in a silk-hose. 40

BRAINWORM

Believe me, Master Stephen, rarely well.

STEPHEN

In sadness, I think it would: I have a reasonable good leg.

BRAINWORM

You have an excellent good leg, Master Stephen, but I cannot stay, to praise it longer now, and I am very sorry for't. [*Exit*] 45

STEPHEN

Another time will serve, Brainworm. Gramercy for this.

ED. KNO'WELL

Ha, ha, ha! ([ED.] KNO'WELL *laughs having read the letter*)

STEPHEN

'Slid, I hope, he laughs not at me, and he do—

27 *no boot* 'no use'. A common Elizabethan pun
28 *truss* to tie the laces ('points') that attached the hose to the doublet
30 *trussed* Brainworm saucily quibbles on the sense of 'beaten'
32 *founder you* bring you to disaster
38 *again* again', F1. 'Again', with or without the apostrophe, was an old form of 'against', 'in anticipation of'
42 *In sadness* 'in all seriousness'
46 *Gramercy* great thanks: grande merci
48 *'Slid* see I.i, 48n.
     and if

35 *woollen stocking*. Queen Elizabeth changed from woollen to silk hose in 1561; this seems to have set the fashion. See *Twelfth Night*, I.iii.

ED. KNO'WELL

Here was a letter, indeed, to be intercepted by a man's
father, and do him good with him! He cannot but think most   50
virtuously, both of me, and the sender, sure; that make the
careful costermonger of him in our 'familiar Epistles'. Well,
if he read this with patience, I'll be gelt, and troll ballads for
Master John Trundle, yonder, the rest of my mortality.
It is true, and likely, my father may have as much patience as   55
another man; for he takes very much physic: and, oft taking
physic makes a man very patient. But would your packet,
Master Wellbred, had arrived at him, in such a minute of
his patience; then, we had known the end of it, which now
is doubtful, and threatens—[*Sees* STEPHEN] What! My wise   60
cousin! [*Aside*] Nay, then, I'll furnish our feast with one
gull more to'ard the mess. He writes to me of a brace, and
here's one, that's three: Oh, for a fourth; Fortune, if ever
thou'lt use thine eyes, I entreat thee—

STEPHEN

[*Aside*] Oh, now I see, who he laughed at. He laughed at   65
somebody in that letter. By this good light, and he had
laughed at me—

ED. KNO'WELL

How now, cousin Stephen, melancholy?

STEPHEN

Yes, a little. I thought, you had laughed at me, cousin.

ED. KNO'WELL

Why, what an' I had coz, what would you ha' done?   70

STEPHEN

By this light, I would ha' told mine uncle.

53 *gelt* castrated
56–57 *physic . . . patient* the sexual meaning of 'physic' ('sexual
attention, intercourse') is played with here, with a weak pun on
'patient'
62 *mess* party; originally a set of four at a banquet
71 *By this light* probably a softening of 'By God's Light' ('Slight)

---

52 *costermonger* (Costar'-monger, F1). Alludes to the care of his apples
(costards) which Wellbred has attributed to Old Kno'well in the letter.
'*familiar Epistles*' italicized in F1. As Herford and Simpson point out,
the use of italic here points to a title, such as the letters of Cicero or Pliny.
53 *troll.* A vivacious style of singing. Ballad singers were looked down upon.
54 *Mr. John Trundle.* Bookseller from 1603 to 1626; published First Quarto
of *Hamlet* in 1603 with Nicholas Ling, but was especially a publisher of
popular ballads; does not appear in Q.
68 *melancholy?* Ed. Kno'well flatters Stephen at the same time as he
mocks him: to be 'melancholy' was an essential aspect of behaviour for
the would-be gallant.

ED. KNO'WELL
Nay, if you would ha' told your uncle, I did laugh at you, coz.
STEPHEN
Did you, indeed?
ED. KNO'WELL
Yes, indeed.
STEPHEN
Why, then—   75
ED. KNO'WELL
What then?
STEPHEN
I am satisfied, it is sufficient.
ED. KNO'WELL
Why, be so gentle coz. And, I pray you let me entreat a
courtesy of you. I am sent for, this morning, by a friend
i' the Old Jewry to come to him; it's but crossing over the   80
fields to Moorgate: will you bear me company? I protest, it
is not to draw you into bond, or any plot against the state,
coz.
STEPHEN
Sir, that's all one, and 'twere: you shall command me, twice
so far as Moorgate to do you good, in such a matter. Do you   85
think I would leave you? I protest—
ED. KNO'WELL
No, no, you shall not protest, coz.
STEPHEN
By my fackins, but I will, by your leave; I'll protest more to
my friend, than I'll speak of, at this time.
ED. KNO'WELL
You speak very well, coz.   90
STEPHEN
Nay, not so neither, you shall pardon me: but I speak, to
serve my turn.
ED. KNO'WELL
Your turn, coz? Do you know, what you say? A gentleman
of your sort, parts, carriage, and estimation, to talk o' your

81 *Moorgate* then a postern-gate in the City wall
86 *protest* a fashionable affectation
88 *By my fackins* by my faith
    protest Stephen apes young Kno'well, quite failing to perceive his
    mockery
92 *turn* obviously considered a vulgarism. Young Kno'well subtly
    expresses his well-bred scorn for the term by punning on it:
    water-carriers referred to a journey as a 'turn', as we see in the
    next scene, I.iii, 52
94 *sort* rank

turn i' this company, and to me, alone, like a tankard-bearer,   95
at a conduit! Fie. A wight, that, hitherto, his every foot
hath left the stamp of a great foot behind him, as every word
the savour of a strong spirit! And he! This man! So graced,
gilded, or—to use a more fit metaphor—so tin-foiled by
nature, as not ten housewives' pewter, again a good time,   100
shows more bright to the world than he! And he—as I said
last, so I say again, and still shall say it—this man! To
conceal such real ornaments as these, and shadow their
glory, as a milliner's wife does her wrought stomacher, with
a smoky lawn, or a black cyprus? Oh coz! It cannot be   105
answered, go not about it. Drake's old ship, at Deptford,
may sooner circle the world again. Come, wrong not the
quality of your desert, with looking downward, coz; but
hold up your head, so: and let the Idea of what you are, be
portrayed i' your face, that men may read i' your physnomy,   110
'Here, within this place, is to be seen the true, rare, and
accomplished monster, or miracle of nature', which is all
one. What think you of this, coz?

STEPHEN

Why, I do think of it; and I will be more proud, and
melancholy, and gentleman-like, than I have been: I'll   115
insure you.

 95 *this company* refers to the audience
100 *pewter* this is of course dull
     good time festive occasion
104 *milliner* (Millaners, F1) originally a trader in fancy goods, especi-
     ally those made in Milan
     wrought stomacher embroidered covering for the breast, worn by
     both sexes
105 *lawn* fine linen material
108 *quality of your desert* what you deserve
109 *Idea* used in the Platonic sense of 'true form'
116 *insure* (ensure, F1) guarantee

95–96 *tankard-bearer, at a conduit.* See *The Persons of the Play*, 14 n.
    Those who carried and sold water were called tankard-bearers.
105 *cyprus.* A delicate transparent kind of crape, almost certainly derived
    from the name of the island, from which many fabrics were bought
    after the Crusades.
106 *Drake's old ship, at Deptford. The Golden Hind*, which had been per-
    manently laid up by order of Queen Elizabeth. It became a holiday
    resort.
110 *physnomy.* A then acceptable form of 'physiognomy': the countenance,
    especially as an index to the character.
112 *monster.* Stephen, unknown to himself, is being compared to a monster
    at an exhibition.
112–113 *all one.* Mockingly echoes Stephen's false gallantry in I.ii, 84, above.

ED. KNO'WELL

Why, that's resolute Master Stephen!
[*Aside*] Now, if I can but hold him up to his height, as it is
happily begun, it will do well for a suburb-humour:
we may hap have a match with the city, and play him   120
for forty pound.—Come, coz.

STEPHEN

I'll follow you.

ED. KNO'WELL

Follow me? You must go before.

STEPHEN

Nay, an' I must, I will. Pray you, show me, good cousin.

[*Exeunt*]

Act I, Scene [iii]

[*The Lane before* COB'S *House*]

[*Enter*] MATTHEW

MATTHEW

I think, this be the house: what, ho?

COB [*opening door*]

COB

Who's there? Oh, Master Matthew! Gi' your worship good
morrow.

MATTHEW

What! Cob! How dost thou, good Cob? Dost thou inhabit
here, Cob?   5

COB

Ay, sir, I and my lineage ha' kept a poor house, here, in our
days.

MATTHEW

Thy lineage, Monsieur Cob, what lineage? What lineage?

COB

Why sir, an ancient lineage, and a princely. Mine ance'try
came from a King's belly, no worse man: and yet no man   10
neither—by your worship's leave, I did lie in that—but

123 *go before* like a serving-man
    Scene [*iii*] Scene iv in Ff

_____

119 *suburb-humour.* Low, unsophisticated humour, as contrasted with the
'Poet-major, o' the town' of Wellbred's letter; Ed. Kno'well intends to
match the country gull against this town gull.

Herring the King of fish, from his belly, I proceed, one o'
the Monarchs o' the world, I assure you. The first red
herring, that was broiled in Adam, and Eve's kitchen, do I
fetch my pedigree from, by the Harrots' books. His cob, was   15
my great-great-mighty-great grandfather.

MATTHEW
Why mighty? Why mighty? I pray thee.

COB
Oh, it was a mighty while ago, sir, and a mighty great cob.

MATTHEW
How know'st thou that?

COB
How know I? Why, I smell his ghost, ever and anon.   20

MATTHEW
Smell a ghost? Oh unsavoury jest! And the ghost of a
herring-cob!

COB
Ay, sir, with favour of your worship's nose, Master
Matthew, why not the ghost of a herring-cob, as well as the
ghost of rasher-bacon?   25

MATTHEW
Roger Bacon, thou would'st say?

12 *Herring the King of fish. Nashes lenten stuffe, the praise of red herring*
(1599), describes how the herring became king of the fish: a hawk was
devoured by a shark, and the birds decided to take revenge; the puffin
(half bird and half fish) betrayed the conspiracy; the fish decided to
elect a King, and 'None won the day in this but the Herring, whom all
their clamorous suffrages saluted with *Vive le roy* . . . and the Herring
ever since wears a coronet on his head, in token that he is as he is'.

13–14 *red herring.* See *Nashes lenten stuffe*: '. . . think on a red Herring,
such a hot stirring meat it is . . . enough to make the cravenest dastard
proclaim fire and sword against Spain. . . .'

15 *Harrots' books.* Harrots bookes, F1, Harrot's book, G, Nn, Sh, N, H, S.
This emendation is inexplicable. *Harrots'* obsolete spelling of 'heralds'.
This alludes to the craze for pedigrees, and to the heralds who 'can give
arms and marks . . .' but 'cannot honour'. (*The Staple of News*, IV.i.)
cob. Originally the head of a red herring; it became a cant term for the
whole fish. Here it means 'young herring', i.e. his son.

26–27 *Roger Bacon . . . coals.* Roger Bacon (?1214–?1297) was a scientist
and philosopher who, although he ran into difficulties with the authorities and was put in close confinement for some ten years, died a natural
death. His popular reputation was, however, as a necromancer who
created a brazen head (see I.iii, 58 below) that talked and 'by the which
he would have walled England about with Brass' (see Robert Greene's
play, *Friar Bacon and Friar Bungay, c.* 1588, published 1594), and it is
not unlikely that a popular chapbook had him burnt. This is the kind
of 'history' with which Cob would be familiar. Sale suggests that Cob
may be confusing 'brazen' with 'brazier'.

COB

I say rasher-bacon. They were both broiled o' the coals?
And a man may smell broiled meat, I hope? You are a
scholar, upsolve me that, now.

MATTHEW

[*Aside*] Oh raw ignorance!—Cob, canst thou show me of a   30
gentleman, one Captain Bobadill, where his lodging is?

COB

Oh, my guest, sir! You mean.

MATTHEW

Thy guest! Alas! Ha, ha.

COB

Why do you laugh, sir? Do you not mean Captain Bobadill?

MATTHEW

Cob, 'pray thee, advise thyself well: do not wrong the   35
gentleman, and thyself too. I dare be sworn, he scorns thy
house: he! He lodge in such a base, obscure place, as thy
house! Tut, I know his disposition so well, he would not
lie in thy bed, if thou'dst gi'it him.

COB

I will not give it him, though, sir. Mass, I thought somewhat   40
was in't, we could not get him to bed, all night! Well, sir,
though he lie not o' my bed, he lies o' my bench: an't please
you to go up, sir, you shall find him with two cushions under
his head, and his cloak wrapped about him, as though he
had neither won nor lost, and yet, I warrant, he ne'er cast   45
better in his life, than he has done, tonight.

MATTHEW

Why? Was he drunk?

COB

Drunk, sir? You hear not me say so. Perhaps, he swallowed
a tavern-token, or some such device, sir: I have nothing to
do withal. I deal with water, and not with wine. Gi'me my   50
tankard there, ho. [*Enter* TIB *with tankard, and exit*] God
b'w'you, sir. It's six o'clock; I should ha' carried two turns,
by this. What ho! My stopple! Come.

29 *upsolve* solve. Almost certainly a vulgarism
40 *Mass* a common oath
45 *cast* a common pun on the two senses of 'to throw dice' and 'to
   vomit'
53 *stopple* stopper

48–49 *swallowed . . . tavern-token.* A cant term for getting drunk: there was
   a shortage of small change in Jonson's time, and tradesmen—including
   innkeepers—issued tokens in lieu; they were issued at the Mermaid in
   Cheapside, where Jonson and his friends met in the earlier period of his
   life.

MATTHEW

Lie in a water-bearer's house! A gentleman of his havings!
Well, I'll tell him my mind.   55

COB

What Tib, show this gentleman up to the Captain. [*Enter
TIB with stopple and exit with MATTHEW*] Oh, an' my house
were the Brazen-head now! Faith, it would e'en speak,
'Moe fools yet'. You should ha' some now would take this
Master Matthew to be a gentleman, at the least. His father's   60
an honest man, a worshipful fishmonger, and so forth; and
now does he creep, and wriggle into acquaintance with all
the brave gallants about the town, such as my guest is—Oh,
my guest is a fine man—and they flout him invincibly. He
useth every day to a merchant's house, where I serve water,   65
one Master Kitely's, i' the Old Jewry; and here's the jest,
he is in love with my master's sister, Mistress Bridget, and
calls her mistress: and there he will sit you a whole after-
noon sometimes, reading o' these same abominable, vile—
a pox on 'hem, I cannot abide them—rascally verses, poyetry,   70
poyetry, and speaking of interludes, 'twill make a man burst
to hear him. And the wenches, they do so jeer, and ti-he at
him—well, should they do so much to me, I'd forswear
them all, by the foot of Pharaoh. There's an oath! How
many water-bearers shall you hear swear such an oath? Oh,   75
I have a guest. He teaches me. He does swear the legiblest,
of any man christened: 'By St. George, the foot of Pharaoh,
the body of me, as I am a gentleman and a soldier': such
dainty oaths! And withal, he does take this same filthy
roguish tobacco, the finest, and cleanliest! It would do a   80
man good to see the fume come forth at's tonnels! Well, he

---

54 *havings* possessions. This replaces 'note' in Q
58 *Brazen-head* see I.iii, 26–27 n.
61 *worshipful fishmonger* member of the city company
64 *invincibly* malapropism for 'invisibly', i.e. 'without his knowing
    it'
65 *useth* 'is in the habit of going to'
72 *ti-he* titter
81 *tonnels* tunnels, i.e. nostrils

---

59 *Moe fools yet.* In the legend (followed by Greene in his play) the head
    says 'Time is', then 'Time was' and finally 'Time is past'; Cob im-
    provises his own facetious version.
70 *poyetry.* An indication of Cob's broad pronunciation.
74 *There's . . . oath.* Gallants made a special study of oaths.
76 *legiblest.* A comic error; writing and speaking are characteristically
    confused by Cob.
80 *the finest and cleanliest.* i.e. Bobadill says this of it.

owes me forty shillings—my wife lent him out of her purse,
by sixpence a time—besides his lodging: I would I had it.
I shall ha'it, he says, the next Action. Helter skelter, hang
sorrow, care'll kill a cat, up-tails all, and a louse for the   85
hangman.

Act I, Scene [iv]

[A Room in COB'S *House]*
BOBAD[ILL] *is discovered lying on his bench*

BOBADILL
Hostess, hostess.

[Enter] TIB

TIB
What say you, sir?
BOBADILL
A cup o' thy small beer, sweet hostess.
TIB
Sir, there's a gentleman, below, would speak with you.
BOBADILL
A gentleman! 'odso, I am not within.   5
TIB
My husband told him you were, sir.
BOBADILL
What a plague—what meant he?
MATTHEW
[Below] Captain Bobadill?
BOBADILL
Who's there?—Take away the basin, good hostess.—Come
up, sir.   10
TIB
He would desire you to come up, sir. You come into a
cleanly house, here.

Scene [iv] Scene v in Ff
5 *'odso* a commonplace oath: 'God's so' ('ods so, F1)
9 *basin* into which he has 'cast'

---

84 *Action.* Military action. Bobadill makes a living by posing as a soldier.
There is some argument as to whether Cob is taken in or not; but his
rueful 'I would I had it' and the string of proverbial expressions that
follows make it clear that he is doubtful.
84–86 *Helter . . . hangman.* A series of popular phrases from songs, games,
etc.
11–12 *You . . . here.* A masterly touch: Jonson perfectly portrays both
plebeian female untruthfulness and house-pride.

[*Enter*] MATTHEW

MATTHEW

'Save you, sir. 'Save you, Captain.

BOBADILL

Gentle Master Matthew! Is it you, sir? Please you sit down.

MATTHEW

Thank you, good Captain, you may see, I am somewhat   15
audacious.

BOBADILL

Not so, sir. I was requested to supper, last night, by a sort of
gallants, where you were wished for, and drunk to, I assure
you.

MATTHEW

Vouchsafe me, by whom, good Captain.   20

BOBADILL

Marry, by young Wellbred, and others. Why, hostess, a stool
here, for this gentleman.

MATTHEW

No haste, sir, 'tis very well.   [*Exit* TIB]

BOBADILL

Body of me! It was so late ere we parted last night, I can
scarce open my eyes, yet; I was but new risen, as you came: 25
how passes the day abroad, sir? You can tell.

MATTHEW

Faith, some half hour to seven: now trust me, you have an
exceeding fine lodging here, very neat, and private!

BOBADILL

Ay, sir: sit down, I pray you. Master Matthew, in any case,
possess no gentleman of our acquaintance, with notice of   30
my lodging.

MATTHEW

Who? I sir? No.

BOBADILL

Not that I need to care who know it, for the cabin is convenient, but in regard I would not be too popular, and
generally visited, as some are.   35

MATTHEW

True, Captain, I conceive you.

BOBADILL

For, do you see, sir, by the heart of valour, in me—except

᛫   17 *sort* company
     20 *Vouchsafe me* another fashionable affectation
     30 *possess* inform
     36 *conceive* understand

33 *cabin*. In military terminology, a tent: Bobadill is playing the soldier.

it be to some peculiar and choice spirits, to whom I am
extraordinarily engaged, as yourself, or so—I could not
extend thus far.   40
MATTHEW

Oh Lord, sir, I resolve so.
BOBADILL

I confess, I love a cleanly and quiet privacy, above all the
tumult, and roar of fortune. What new book ha' you there?
What! 'Go by, Hieronymo'?
MATTHEW

Ay, did you ever see it acted? Is't not well penned?   45
BOBADILL

Well penned? I would fain see all the poets, of these times,
pen such another play as that was! They'll prate and swagger,
and keep a stir of art and devices, when, as I am a gentleman, read 'hem, they are the most shallow, pitiful, barren
fellows, that live upon the face of the earth, again!   50
MATTHEW

Indeed, here are a number of fine speeches in this book!
'Oh eyes, no eyes, but fountains fraught with tears'! There's
a conceit! 'Fountains fraught with tears'! 'O life, no life,
but lively form of death'! Another! 'Oh world, no world,
but mass of public wrongs'! A third! 'Confused and filled   55
with murder and misdeeds'! A fourth! Oh, the Muses! Is't not
excellent? Is't not simply the best that ever you heard,
Captain? Ha? How do you like it?
BOBADILL

'Tis good.

---

50 *again!* here an exclamation denoting emphasis

44 *'Go by, Hieronymo'*. The book referred to is Thomas Kyd's *The Spanish
   Tragedy*, identified here by the most often used quotation from it.
   Jonson's attitude to it here is not altogether deprecatory—there is some
   affection in his mockery of Matthew's admiration of it, which would
   have been regarded as old-fashioned and ignorant. In 1601 Jonson
   received money from Henslowe via Edward Alleyn to write additions
   to *The Spanish Tragedy*, although these are probably not the ones that
   appear in the 1602 edition of this play. It has been suggested that
   Jonson was taking a risk in putting his own opinions into the mouth of
   a gull; but he is not doing this: he is showing how the pseudo-gallant
   and 'poet o' the town' talked about Kyd's play—his own affection for
   it is beside the point. If one parodies an old-fashioned schoolmaster
   voicing platitudinous praise of Shakespeare by quoting stock lines, one
   is not criticizing Shakespeare.
52-56 All the quotations are from *The Spanish Tragedy*.

MATTHEW

> *To thee, the purest object to my sense,*   60
> *The most refined essence heaven covers,*
> *Send I these lines, wherein I do commence*
> *The happy state of turtle-billing lovers.*
> *If they prove rough, unpolished, harsh and rude,*
> *Haste made the waste. Thus, mildly, I conclude.*   65

> BOBADILL *is making him ready all this while*

BOBADILL

Nay, proceed, proceed. Where's this?

MATTHEW

This, sir? A toy o' mine own, in my nonage: the infancy of
my Muses! But, when will you come and see my study?
Good faith, I can show you some very good things, I have
done of late— That boot becomes your leg, passing well,   70
Captain, methinks!

BOBADILL

So, so; it's the fashion, gentlemen now use.

MATTHEW

Troth, Captain, an' now you speak o' the fashion, Master
Wellbred's elder brother, and I, are fall'n out exceedingly:
this other day, I happened to enter into some discourse of   75
a hanger, which I assure you, both for fashion, and work-
manship, was most peremptory-beautiful, and gentleman-
like! Yet, he condemned, and cried it down, for the most
pied, and ridiculous that ever he saw.

BOBADILL

Squire Downright? The half-brother? Was't not?   80

MATTHEW

Ay, sir, he.

BOBADILL

Hang him, rook, he! Why, he has no more judgement than a
malt-horse. By St. George, I wonder you'd lose a thought
upon such an animal: the most peremptory absurd clown of
Christendom, this day, he is holden. I protest to you, as I   85
am a gentleman, and a soldier, I ne'er changed words, with
his like. By his discourse, he should eat nothing but hay.

s.d. *making him ready* dressing
76 *hanger* the loop in the belt from which the sword was hung
77 *peremptory*—a common intensive
79 *pied* variegated, i.e., 'fancy; precious'
82 *rook* simpleton
83 *malt-horse* dray-horse

60–65 A parody of insincere and ineffective love poetry, perhaps with a
glance at Samuel Daniel.

He was born for the manger, pannier, or pack-saddle! He
has not so much as a good phrase in his belly, but all old
iron, and rusty proverbs! A good commodity for some   90
smith, to make hobnails of.

MATTHEW

Ay, and he thinks to carry it away with his manhood still,
where he comes. He brags he will gi' me the bastinado, as I
hear.

BOBADILL

How! He the bastinado! How came he by that word, trow?   95

MATTHEW

Nay, indeed, he said cudgel me; I termed it so, for my more
grace.

BOBADILL

That may be: for I was sure, it was none of his word. But,
when? When said he so?

MATTHEW

Faith, yesterday, they say: a young gallant, a friend of mine   100
told me so.

BOBADILL

By the foot of Pharaoh, and 'twere my case now, I should
send him a chartel, presently. The bastinado! A most
proper, and sufficient dependence, warranted by the great
Caranza. Come hither. You shall chartel him. I'll show you a   105
trick, or two, you shall kill him with, at pleasure: the first
stoccata, if you will, by this air.

MATTHEW

Indeed, you have absolute knowledge i' the mystery, I have
heard, sir.

BOBADILL

Of whom? Of whom ha' you heard it, I beseech you?   110

MATTHEW

Troth, I have heard it spoken of divers, that you have very
rare, and un-in-one-breath-utter-able skill, sir.

BOBADILL

By heaven, no, not I; no skill i' the earth: some small rudi-
ments i' the science, as to know my time, distance, or so.
I have professed it more for noblemen, and gentlemen's use,   115

---

 93 *bastinado* a beating with a cudgel
103 *chartel* challenge to a duel
     presently instantly
104 *dependence* reason for quarrel—a duelling term
107 *stoccata* thrust

---

105 *Caranza.* Jeronimo de Caranza, author of a work on the philosophy and
     etiquette of duelling.

than mine own practice, I assure you. Hostess, accommodate
us with another bed-staff here, quickly. [*Enter* TIB *with a
puzzled air*] Lend us another bed-staff. [*Exit* TIB] The
woman does not understand the words of Action. Look you,
sir. Exalt not your point above this state, at any hand, and   120
let your poniard maintain your defence, thus. [*Enter* TIB
with bed-staff] Give it to the gentleman, and leave us. [*Exit*
TIB] So, sir. Come on: Oh, twine your body more about,
that you may fall to a more sweet comely gentleman-like
guard. So, indifferent. Hollow your body more sir, thus.   125
Now, stand fast o' your left leg, note your distance, keep
your due proportion of time— Oh, you disorder your point,
most irregularly!

MATTHEW
How is the bearing of it, now, sir?

BOBADILL
Oh, out of measure ill! A well-experienced hand would   130
pass upon you, at pleasure.

MATTHEW
How mean you, sir, pass upon me?

BOBADILL
Why, thus sir. Make a thrust at me. Come in, upon the
answer, control your point, and make a full career, at the
body. The best-practised gallants of the time, name it the   135
passada: a most desperate thrust, believe it!

MATTHEW
Well, come, sir.

BOBADILL
Why, you do not manage your weapon with any facility,

119 *words of Action* refers to 'accommodate' in l. 116
120 *state* an affected word for 'position'
    at any hand 'in any circumstances'
127-128 *disorder . . . irregularly* 'you do not hold your sword accord-
    ing to the rules'
136 *passada* a thrust made while the swordsman advances one foot
    forward

---

116 *accommodate*. Jonson condemned this word as an affectation (one of
    'the perfumed terms of the time') in *Discoveries*.
117 *bed-staff*. A variously used term; here it refers to a stick about the size
    of a sword which was used for beating and smoothing the bed when it
    was being made.
121 *poinard . . . defence*. Elizabethan duelling involved holding a dagger in
    the left hand as well as a sword in the right.
138-140 *Why . . . tedious*. Bobadill carefully avoids any actual test of his
    skill, even with Matthew.

3—EMIHH

or grace to invite me: I have no spirit to play with you. Your
dearth of judgement renders you tedious.   140

MATTHEW

But one venue, sir.

BOBADILL

Venue! Fie. Most gross denomination, as ever I heard. Oh,
the stoccata, while you live, sir. Note that. Come, put on
your cloak, and we'll go to some private place, where you
are acquainted, some tavern, or so—and have a bit—I'll   145
send for one of these Fencers, and he shall breath you, by
my direction; and, then, I will teach you your trick. You shall
kill him with it, at the first, if you please. Why, I will learn
you, by the true judgement of the eye, hand, and foot, to
control any enemy's point i' the world. Should your adver-   150
sary confront you with a pistol, 'twere nothing, by this hand,
you should, by the same rule, control his bullet, in a line:
except it were hail-shot, and spread. What money ha' you
about you, Master Matthew?

MATTHEW

Faith, I ha' not past a two shillings, or so.   155

BOBADILL

'Tis somewhat with the least: but, come. We will have a
bunch of radish, and salt, to taste our wine; and a pipe of
tobacco, to close the orifice of the stomach: and then, we'll
call upon young Wellbred. Perhaps we shall meet the
Corydon, his brother, there: and put him to the question.   160

Act II, Scene i

The Old Jewry [*A Hall in* KITELY's *House*]

[*Enter*] KITELY, CASH [*and*] DOWNRIGHT

KITELY

Thomas, come hither,
There lies a note, within upon my desk,
Here, take my key: it is no matter, neither.
Where is the boy?

CASH   Within, sir, i' the warehouse.

---

148 *him* i.e. Downright

---

142 *venue.* Thrust; Bobadill sneers at Matthew's unfashionable use of the
     French term.
160 *Corydon.* Regarded by Jonson and his contemporaries as the prototype
     of bucolic boorishness. He occurs in Theocritus's *Idylls,* and Vergil
     uses the name for a shepherd in *Eclogues* 2 and 7, but with no suggestions
     of boorishness.

KITELY

   Let him tell over, straight, that Spanish gold,   5
   And weigh it, with th' pieces of eight. Do you
   See the delivery of those silver stuffs,
   To Master Lucar. Tell him, if he will,
   He shall ha' the grograns, at the rate I told him,
   And I will meet him, on the Exchange, anon.   10

CASH

   Good, sir.   [*Exit*]

KITELY   Do you see that fellow, brother Downright?

DOWNRIGHT

   Ay, what of him?

KITELY   He is a jewel, brother.

   I took him of a child, up, at my door,
   And christened him, gave him mine own name, Thomas,
   Since bred him at the Hospital; where proving   15
   A toward imp, I called him home, and taught him
   So much, as I have made him my cashier,
   And given him, who had none, a surname, Cash:
   And find him, in his place so full of faith,
   That, I durst trust my life into his hands.   20

DOWNRIGHT

   So, would not I in any bastard's, brother,
   As, it is like, he is: although I knew
   Myself his father. But you said you'd somewhat
   To tell me, gentle brother, what is't? What is't?

KITELY

   Faith, I am very loath, to utter it,   25
   As fearing, it may hurt your patience:
   But, that I know, your judgement is of strength,
   Against the nearness of affection—

  9 *grograns* a coarse, ribbed material consisting of silk mixed with
     mohair or wool
 13 *of* when
 15 *the Hospital* Christ's Hospital, the Blue Coat school
 20 *my life into his hands* 'but not his *key*!' (Sale)
 23 *you'd* yo' had, F1
 27 *But* both, G, Sh, N, H, S

---

  6 *with th'*. 'Only Jonson's meticulous way of writing "wi' the" ' (Herford
    and Simpson).
    pieces of eight. Money coined by Queen Elizabeth for trade with the
    Indies, valued at four shillings and sixpence; it was equivalent to the
    Spanish dollar, or 'piece of eight reals'.
 10 *Exchange*. The Royal Exchange, which after the Queen's visit there in
    1570 was popular as a place of trade and as a fashionable resort for
    idlers.

DOWNRIGHT
  What need this circumstance? Pray you be direct.
KITELY
  I will not say, how much I do ascribe   30
  Unto your friendship; nor, in what regard
  I hold your love: but, let my past behaviour,
  And usage of your sister, but confirm
  How well I've been affected to your—
DOWNRIGHT
  You are too tedious, come to the matter, the matter.   35
KITELY
  Then, without further ceremony, thus.
  My brother Wellbred, sir, I know not how,
  Of late, is much declined in what he was,
  And greatly altered in his disposition.
  When he came first to lodge here in my house,   40
  Ne'er trust me, if I were not proud of him:
  Methought he bare himself in such a fashion,
  So full of man, and sweetness in his carriage,
  And, what was chief, it showed not borrowed in him,
  But all he did, became him as his own,   45
  And seemed as perfect, proper, and possessed
  As breath, with life, or colour, with the blood.
  But, now, his course is so irregular,
  So loose, affected, and deprived of grace,
  And he himself withal so far fall'n off   50
  From that first place, as scarce no note remains,
  To tell men's judgements where he lately stood.
  He's grown a stranger to all due respect,
  Forgetful of his friends, and not content
  To stale himself in all societies,   55
  He makes my house here common, as a mart,
  A theatre, a public receptacle
  For giddy humour, and diseased riot;
  And here, as in a tavern, or a stews,
  He, and his wild associates, spend their hours,   60
  In repetition of lascivious jests,
  Swear, leap, drink, dance, and revel night by night,
  Control my servants: and indeed what not?
DOWNRIGHT
  'Sdeins, I know not what I should say to him, i' the whole

55 *stale* make himself cheap   59 *stews* brothel

---

64 *'Sdeins.* Short for 'God's deynes' or 'dines'. *O.E.D.* suggests that
  'dines' is a corruption of 'dignesse', so that the phrase means 'by God's
  dignity', but Herford and Simpson do not agree. Others explain it as
  'disdain', and N conjectures 'God's veins'.

world! He values me, at a cracked three-farthings, for aught   65
I see: it will never out o' the flesh that's bred i' the bone! I
have told him enough, one would think, if that would serve:
but counsel to him, is as good, as a shoulder of mutton to a
sick horse. Well! He knows what to trust to, for George.
Let him spend, and spend, and domineer, till his heart ache;   70
an' he think to be relieved by me, when he is got into one o'
your city pounds, the Counters, he has the wrong sow by
the ear, i' faith: and claps his dish at the wrong man's door.
I'll lay my hand o' my halfpenny, ere I part with't, to fetch
him out, I'll assure him.   75

KITELY
Nay, good brother, let it not trouble you, thus.

DOWNRIGHT
'Sdeath, he mads me, I could eat my very spur-leathers, for
anger! But, why are you so tame? Why do you not speak to
him, and tell him how he disquiets your house?

KITELY
Oh, there are divers reasons to dissuade, brother.   80
But, would yourself vouchsafe to travail in it,
Though but with plain, and easy circumstance,
It would, both come much better to his sense,
And savour less of stomach, or of passion.
You are his elder brother, and that title   85
Both gives, and warrants you authority;
Which, by your presence seconded, must breed

66–69 a series of 'rusty proverbs' (see I.iv, 90)
80 *dissuade, brother* dissuade me, Q, G, Sh, H, S
81 *travail in it* undertake it
84 *stomach* anger

---

65 *cracked three-farthings*. Three-farthings were coined between 1561 and
  1582. They were of silver so thin that they were liable to crack.
69 *for George*. The same as 'by St. George', used by Bobadill (I.iv, 83).
  'For' is here a corruption of ''fore'.
72 *Counters*. The two City of London prisons, in Wood Street and
  Poultry.
72–73 Two more 'rusty proverbs'. Beggars attracted attention by clapping
  a wooden dish (for the alms they received) with a cover; however,
  beadles and other parish officers also sometimes solicited in this way for
  the relief of the poor or diseased.
74 *I'll . . . halfpenny*. Another proverb, which meant 'to have a particular
  object in view'. Downright plays on rather than uses it.
82 *Though . . . circumstance*. Kitely is digging at Downright in return for
  his remarks about his own tediousness—the line has the force of
  'you're not so straightforward yourself: you have your faults'. 'Easy'
  here implies 'temperate'.

A kind of duty in him, and regard:
Whereas, if I should intimate the least,
It would but add contempt, to his neglect,   90
Heap worse on ill, make up a pile of hatred
That, in the rearing, would come tottering down,
And, in the ruin, bury all our love.
Nay, more than this, brother, if I should speak
He would be ready from his heat of humour,   95
And overflowing of the vapour, in him,
To blow the ears of his familiars,
With the false breath, of telling, what disgraces,
And low disparagements, I had put upon him.
Whilst they, sir, to relieve him, in the fable,   100
Make their loose comments, upon every word,
Gesture, or look, I use; mock me all over,
From my flat cap, unto my shining shoes:
And, out of their impetuous rioting fant'sies,
Beget some slander, that shall dwell with me.   105
And what would that be, think you? Marry, this.
They would give out, because my wife is fair,
Myself but lately married, and my sister
Here sojourning a virgin in my house,
That I were jealous! Nay, as sure as death,   110
That they would say. And how that I had quarrelled
My brother purposely, thereby to find
An apt pretext, to banish them my house.
DOWNRIGHT
Mass perhaps so: they're like enough to do it.
KITELY
Brother, they would, believe it: so should I,   115

96 *vapour* dejection; 'spleen'

89–93 These lines bring out Kitely's essential kindliness, in contrast to his
    irrational humour. In just the same way, Downright, despite the
    obsessive aspect of his conversation in quoting proverbs, is not alto-
    gether without wit in his use of them. These touches help to make
    Jonson's characters credible, and to distinguish his comedy from the
    cruder form of pure farce.
103 *flat cap* . . . *shining shoes*. Both characteristics of the bourgeois trader,
    as opposed to the more sophisticated citizen. By 1597 more extravagant
    headwear had become fashionable. *shining shoes*. i.e. blackened.
107–110 *They* . . . *jealous!* A perfect example of the innocent manner—and
    here Jonson anticipates the psychology of the Twentieth Century—in
    which someone can enunciate his guilty awareness of his own less
    pleasant or irrational characteristics. This is more than merely comic—it
    is shrewd psychology.

Like one of these penurious quack-salvers,
But set the bills up, to mine own disgrace,
And try experiments upon myself:
Lend scorn and envy, opportunity,
To stab my reputation, and good name—   120

[*Enter*] MATTHEW [*struggling with*] BOBADILL

MATTHEW
I will speak to him—
BOBADILL
Speak to him? Away, by the foot of Pharaoh, you shall not,
you shall not do him that grace. The time of day, to you,
gentleman o' the house. Is Master Wellbred stirring?
DOWNRIGHT
How then? What should he do?   125
BOBADILL
Gentleman of the house, it is to you: is he within, sir?
KITELY
He came not to his lodging tonight sir, I assure you.
DOWNRIGHT
Why, do you hear? You!
BOBADILL
The gentleman-citizen hath satisfied me, I'll talk to no
scavenger.   [*Exeunt* MATTHEW *and* BOBADILL]   130
DOWNRIGHT
How, scavenger? Stay sir, stay.
KITELY
Nay, brother Downright.
DOWNRIGHT
'Heart! Stand you away, and you love me.
KITELY
You shall not follow him now, I pray you, brother, good
faith you shall not: I will overrule you.   135
DOWNRIGHT
Ha? Scavenger? Well, go to, I say little: but, by this good day
—God forgive me I should swear—if I put it up so, say, I am
the rankest cow, that ever pissed. 'Sdeins, and I swallow this,
I'll ne'er draw my sword in the sight of Fleet Street again,

121 Begins Scene ii in Ff
139 *Fleet Street* notorious for brawling

116–117 Quacks and sellers of patent medicines put up bills advertising the
     virtues of their wares.
137 *God . . . swear.* Downright chooses to apologize for a much milder oath
     than the ones he usually gives vent to, a typically middle-class habit.

while I live: I'll sit in a barn, with madge-howlet, and catch   140
mice first. Scavenger? 'Heart, and I'll go ne'er to fill that
huge tumbrel-slop of yours, with somewhat, and I have good
luck: your Gargantua breech cannot carry it away so.

KITELY
Oh do not fret yourself thus, never think on't.

DOWNRIGHT
These are my brother's consorts, these! These are his   145
cam'rades, his walking mates! He's a gallant, a cavaliero too,
right hangman cut! Let me not live, and I could not find in
my heart to swinge the whole ging of 'hem, one after
another, and begin with him first. I am grieved, it should be
said he is my brother, and take these courses. Well, as he   150
brews, so he shall drink, for George, again. Yet, he shall
hear on't, and that tightly too, and I live, i' faith.

KITELY
But, brother, let your reprehension, then,
Run in an easy current, not o'er high
Carried with rashness, or devouring choler;   155
But rather use the soft persuading way,
Whose powers will work more gently, and compose
Th'imperfect thoughts you labour to reclaim:
More winning, than enforcing the consent.

DOWNRIGHT
Ay, ay, let me alone for that, I warrant you.   [*Bell rings*]   160

KITELY
How now? Oh, the bell rings to breakfast.
Brother, I pray you go in, and bear my wife
Company, till I come; I'll but give order
For some despatch of business to my servants—
                              [*Exit* DOWNRIGHT]

COB *passes by with his tankard*

140 *madge-howlet* madge was a popular name for the owl
147 *right hangman cut* dressed for the hangman
148 *ging* company, usually less disparaging than 'gang'
160 *let . . . that* 'rely on me for that'

---

142 *tumbrel-slop.* Wide breeches, then somewhat in fashion—elsewhere
   referred to by Jonson as 'bombard slops'.
143 *Gargantua.* The reference is unlikely to be to Rabelais's *Gargantua*
   (1535), then little known, but to the giant-hero of a folk-tale.
148 *swinge* Q, F1. Swing, Nn, because of the hangman reference; but
   'swinge' in its familar meaning of 'beat' seems to be correct.
153–159 *But . . . consent.* While Downright is obsessed in his rage against
   Bobadill, Kitely is concerned with his own wish, that Downright should
   take over the difficult task of upbraiding Wellbred.

KITELY
    What Cob? Our maids will have you by the back,   165
    I'faith, for coming so late this morning.

COB
    Perhaps so, sir, take heed somebody have not them by the
    belly, for walking so late in the evening.   [*Exit* COB]

KITELY
    Well, yet my troubled spirit's somewhat eased,
    Though not reposed in that security,   170
    As I could wish: but, I must be content.
    Howe'er I set a face on't to the world,
    Would I had lost this finger, at a venture,
    So Wellbred had ne'er lodged within my house.
    Why't cannot be, where there is such resort   175
    Of wanton gallants, and young revellers,
    That any woman should be honest long.
    Is't like, that factious beauty will preserve
    The public weal of chastity, unshaken,
    When such strong motives muster, and make head   180
    Against her single peace? No, no. Beware,
    When mutual appetite doth meet to treat,
    And spirits of one kind, and quality,
    Come once to parley, in the pride of blood:
    It is no slow conspiracy, that follows.   185
    Well, to be plain, if I but thought, the time
    Had answered their affections: all the world

165 Begins Scene iii in Ff
180 *make head* gather their forces
184 *the pride of blood* the full flush of passion
186–187 *if . . . affections* 'if I thought the opportunity they desired had
    presented itself'

165–166 *What . . . morning.* These lines are printed by most editors as
    prose. The Folio prints them as verse, but with 166 beginning at 'For'.
    I follow Herford and Simpson in regularizing them as verse.
171–172 *As . . . world.* So Ff, but G emended to 'As . . . content,/ . . .
    world.' and has been followed in all editions except by H & S. Q reads
    'content, . . . world,'; being so much more lightly punctuated, it is not
    very helpful here. G's emendation presents grave difficulties: it does
    not make sense that Kitely should admit, even to himself, that he
    appears discontented in the eyes of the world. I follow H & S. Kitely
    means, 'Whatever my preferences may appear to be, I'd rather have
    lost a finger by an accident ("at a venture"=by a mischance) than have
    had Wellbred and his friends here to torture me with jealousy'.
178 *like* likely
    factious. Given to intrigue; Kitely's thus pejorative view of beauty in
    itself is psychologically significant.

Should not persuade me, but I were a cuckold.
Marry, I hope, they ha' not got that start:
For opportunity hath baulked 'hem yet,   190
And shall do still, while I have eyes, and ears
To attend the impositions of my heart.
My presence shall be as an iron bar,
'Twixt the conspiring motions of desire:
Yea, every look, or glance, mine eye ejects,   195
Shall check occasion, as one doth his slave,
When he forgets the limits of prescription.

[*Enter*] DAME KITELY [*and* BRIDGET]

DAME KITELY
Sister Bridget, pray you fetch down the rosewater above in
the closet. [*Exit* BRIDGET] Sweetheart, will you come in, to
breakfast?   200
KITELY
[*Aside*] An' she have overheard me now?
DAME KITELY
I pray thee, good muss, we stay for you.
KITELY
[*Aside*] By heaven I would not for a thousand angels!
DAME KITELY
What ail you sweetheart, are you not well? Speak good muss.
KITELY
Troth, my head aches extremely, on a sudden.   205
DAME KITELY
[*Putting her hand to his forehead*] Oh, the Lord!
KITELY
How now? What?
DAME KITELY
Alas, how it burns! Muss, keep you warm, good truth it is

198 *rosewater* was eaten with fruit
202 *muss* an endearment (mouse)

195 *mine eye ejects*. This gives a striking clue to the sexual neurosis of
repressed voyeurism from which Kitely suffers: the 'iron bar' of l. 193
combines with the 'ejects' (changed from 'objects' in Q) in an actively
phallic image—but Kitely really wants to enjoy sexual fulfilment
through his 'eye' (which he associates directly with his penis, the
instrument of sexual pleasure), by watching.
197 *When . . . prescription*. 'When he forgets his place': the supposed
situation between Dame Kitely and Wellbred and his friends is compared to a 'slave'; the fact that the image is of the slave forgetting his
place (i.e. a sexual fantasy getting out of hand) reinforces the notion of
Kitely's hidden voyeuristic motivation.

this new disease! There's a number are troubled withal! For
love's sake, sweetheart, come in, out of the air.   210

KITELY

[*Aside*] How simple, and how subtle are her answers!
A new disease, and many troubled with it!
Why, true: she heard me, all the world to nothing.

DAME KITELY

I pray thee, good sweetheart, come in; the air will do you
harm, in troth.   215

KITELY

[*Aside*] The air! She has me i' the wind!
Sweetheart!—I'll come to you presently: 'twill away, I hope.

DAME KITELY

Pray heaven it do.   [*Exit* DAME KITELY]

KITELY

A new disease? I know not, new, or old,
But it may well be called poor mortals' plague: 220
For, like a pestilence, it doth infect
The houses of the brain. First, it begins
Solely to work upon the fantasy,
Filling her seat with such pestiferous air,
As soon corrupts the judgement; and from thence   225
Sends like contagion to the memory:
Still each to other giving the infection.
Which, as a subtle vapour, spreads itself,
Confusedly, through every sensive part,
Till not a thought, or motion, in the mind,   230
Be free from the black poison of suspect.
Ah, but what misery' is it, to know this?

---

223 *fantasy* imagination, the foremost 'house of the brain'
225 *judgement* i.e. reason, the middle 'house of the brain'
229 *sensive* sensitive

---

209 *this new disease.* A popular term for any fever the doctors could not
name.
214–215 *the . . . harm.* Fresh air was supposed to be bad for sick people.
216 *She . . . wind!* 'She knows what I'm thinking': in hunting, game was
said to have the hunters 'in the wind' if they approached it from the
windward.
219 *disease.* Here Kitely is speaking with insight, of his own jealousy; the
imagery betrays its sexually neurotic nature.
222 *houses of the brain.* The old anatomical division of the brain was into
three ventricles or 'houses': imagination in front, reason in the middle,
memory at the back.

Or, knowing it, to want the mind's erection,
In such extremes? Well, I will once more strive,
In spite of this black cloud, myself to be,   235
And shake the fever off, that thus shakes me.   [*Exit*]

Act II, Scene ii

[*Moorfields*]

[*Enter*] BRAINWORM [*like a maimed sub-officer*]

BRAINWORM

'Slid, I cannot choose but laugh, to see myself translated
thus, from a poor creature to a creator; for now must I
create an intolerable sort of lies, or my present profession
loses the grace: and yet the lie to a man of my coat, is as
ominous a fruit, as the fico. Oh sir, it holds for good polity   5
ever, to have that outwardly in vilest estimation, that
inwardly is most dear to us. So much, for my borrowed
shape. Well, the troth is, my old master intends to follow
my young, dry foot, over Moorfields, to London, this
morning: now I, knowing, of this hunting-match, or rather   10
conspiracy, and to insinuate with my young master—for so

    Scene ii Scene iv in Ff
 11 *conspiracy* plot (not used here in its more modern sense of 'plot
    hatched between people')
    insinuate ingratiate myself with

---

233 *erection*. Excitement—but also a pun on the sexual meaning, harking
    back to the phallic images of the iron bar and the ejecting eye. These
    lines (233–236) show Kitely becoming aware of his condition: 'How
    miserable am I in fact when I realize that they want each other sexually?
    I need (sexually) the mental excitement fostered by this morbid
    suspicion'. The 'black cloud' is less the jealousy itself than the morbid
    and neurotic reasons for it.
s.d. Moorfields stretched from the City Wall, between Bishopsgate and
    Cripplegate, to Finsbury and Holywell. It was a noted haunt of soldier-
    beggars, many fake, some genuine.
  2–5 *for . . . fico*. The charge of lying was supposed to be intolerable to a
    true soldier *ominous* deadly *fico* 'to give the fico' (fig) was a gesture of
    contempt: one put the thumb between the forefingers or swelled the
    cheek by putting it into the mouth; or the allusion may be only to the
    proverbial poisoned fig of Spain (used to murder someone).
  5–7 *Oh . . . us*. Cf. Kitely's 'detestation' of the notion of sexual connection
    between his wife and Wellbred or his friends.
  9 *dry foot*. By scent—a hunting term meaning to follow the game only by
    scent; but a wicked pun is intended, since Moorfields was marshy at
    that time.

must we that are blue-waiters, and men of hope and service
do, or perhaps we may wear motely at the year's end, and
who wears motley, you know—have got me afore, in this
disguise, determining here to lie in ambuscado, and inter-   15
cept him, in the mid-way. If I can but get his cloak, his
purse, his hat, nay, anything, to cut him off, that is, to say
his journey, veni, vidi, vici, I may say with Captain Caesar,
I am made for ever, i' faith. Well, now must I practise to get
the true garb of one of these lance-knights, my arm here,   20
and my—young master! And his cousin, Master Stephen, as
I am true counterfeit man of war, and no soldier!

                                              [*Moves away*]

          [*Enter*] ED. KNO'WELL [*and*] STEPHEN

ED. KNO'WELL
  So sir, and how then, coz?
STEPHEN
  'Sfoot, I have lost my purse, I think.
ED. KNO'WELL
  How? Lost your purse? Where? When had you it?   25
STEPHEN
  I cannot tell. Stay!
BRAINWORM
  [*Aside*] 'Slid, I am afeared, they will know me, would I could
  get by them.
ED. KNO'WELL
  What? Ha' you it?
STEPHEN
  No, I think I was bewitched, I—   30
ED. KNO'WELL
  Nay, do not weep the loss, hang it, let it go.
STEPHEN
  Oh, it's here: no, and it had been lost, I had not cared, but
  for a jet ring Mistress Mary sent me.

  12 *blue-waiters* servants wore blue
  15 *ambuscado* ambush
  20 *lance-knights* mercenary footsoldiers
  33 *jet ring* a favourite material for cheap rings

  13–14 *or . . . know*. Servants who had offended were sometimes made to
    wear motley, the traditional fool's costume; Brainworm means that if he
    does not support his young master he may fall into disfavour with him
    at his old master's death.
  18 *veni, vidi, vici*. Caesar's boast, or the boast attributed to him, when he
    defeated Pharnaces at Zela in 47 B.C., alluded to as a 'thrasonical brag'
    by Rosalind in *As You Like It* (written *c*. 1598–1599).

ED. KNO'WELL

A jet ring? Oh, the poesy, the poesy?

STEPHEN

Fine, i' faith! 'Though fancy sleep, my love is deep.' Mean-   35
ing that though I did not fancy her, yet she loved me deeply.

ED. KNO'WELL

Most excellent!

STEPHEN

And then, I sent her another, and my poesy was: 'The
deeper, the sweeter, I'll be judged by St. Peter.'

ED. KNO'WELL

How, by St. Peter? I do not conceive that!   40

STEPHEN

Marry, St. Peter, to make up the metre.

ED. KNO'WELL

Well, there the saint was your good patron, he helped you at
your need: thank him, thank him.

BRAINWORM

[*Aside*] I cannot take leave on 'hem, so: I will venture, come
what will. [*Goes towards them*] Gentlemen, please you change   45
a few crowns, for a very excellent good blade, here? I am a
poor gentleman, a soldier, one that, in the better state of my
fortunes, scorned so mean a refuge, but now it is the humour
of necessity, to have it so. You seem to be gentlemen, well
affected to martial men, else I should rather die with   50
silence, than live with shame: however, vouchsafe to
remember, it is my want speaks, not myself. This condition
agrees not with my spirit—

ED. KNO'WELL

Where hast thou served?

BRAINWORM

May it please you, sir, in all the late wars of Bohemia,   55
Hungaria, Dalmatia, Poland, where not, sir? I have been a

---

s.d. [*Goes towards them.*] He is come back, F1

34 *poesy*. i.e. the posy, the engraved rhyming motto. Probably when jet
rings were thus engraved they were lined with silver.

35–36 *Meaning . . . deeply*. Stephen's consummate idiocy is well shown
here.

45–53 *Gentleman . . . spirit*. Brainworm's speech burlesques the Euphuistic
style of the professional beggar who pretends to have known (or
perhaps has known) better days. The skilful patter of the 'pathetic'
'ex-officer', door-to-door brush-salesman in our own day employs
similar devices.

55–56 *Bohemia, Hungaria, Dalmatia, Poland*. There had been continuous
fighting in these countries during the twenty-five years before the first
production of this play.

poor servitor, by sea and land, any time this fourteen years,
and followed the fortunes of the best commanders in
Christendom. I was twice shot at the taking of Aleppo, once
at the relief of Vienna; I have been at Marseilles, Naples,   60
and the Adriatic gulf, a gentleman-slave in the galleys,
thrice, where I was most dangerously shot in the head,
through both the thighs, and yet, being thus maimed, I am
void of maintenance, nothing left me but my scars, the
noted marks of my resolution.   65

STEPHEN
How will you sell this rapier, friend? [*Takes it in his hand*]

BRAINWORM
Generous sir, I refer it to your own judgement; you are a
gentleman, give me what you please.

STEPHEN
True, I am a gentleman, I know that friend: but what
though? I pray you say, what would you ask?   70

BRAINWORM
I assure you, the blade may become the side, or thigh of the
best prince, in Europe.

ED. KNO'WELL
Ay, with a velvet scabbard, I think.

STEPHEN
Nay, and't be mine, it shall have a velvet scabbard, coz, that's
flat: I'd not wear it as 'tis, and you would give me an angel.   75

BRAINWORM
At your worship's pleasure, sir: [STEPHEN *examines the
blade*] nay, 'tis a most pure Toledo.

STEPHEN
I had rather it were a Spaniard! But tell me, what shall I
give you for it? An' it had a silver hilt—

ED. KNO'WELL
Come, come, you shall not buy it; hold, there's a shilling   80
fellow, take thy rapier.

STEPHEN
Why, but I will buy it now, because you say so, and there's
another shilling, fellow. I scorn to be outbidden. What,

66 *How will you sell* 'how much do you want for'
77 *Toledo* Toledo blades were renowned for their excellence
78 *Spaniard* Stephen's knowledge of geography is minimal

59–60 *taking of Aleppo . . . relief of Vienna.* Brainworm suddenly ranges
    back to 1516 and 1529; his next claims are similarly extravagant.
73 *velvet scabbard.* An extravagant fashion of the time, noted in Stubbes's
    Anatomy of Abuses (1583).

shall I walk with a cudgel, like Higginbottom? And may have
a rapier, for money?   85

ED. KNO'WELL

You may buy one in the city.

STEPHEN

Tut, I'll buy this i' the field, so I will, I have a mind to't,
because 'tis a field rapier. Tell me your lowest price.

ED. KNO'WELL

You shall not buy it, I say.

STEPHEN

By this money, but I will, though I give more than 'tis worth.   90

ED. KNO'WELL

Come away, you are a fool.

STEPHEN

Friend, I am a fool, that's granted: but I'll have it, for that
word's sake. Follow me, for your money.

BRAINWORM

At your service, sir.   [*Exeunt*]

Act II, Scene [iii]

[*Another Part of Moorfields*]

[*Enter*] KNO'WELL

KNO'WELL

I cannot lose the thought, yet, of this letter,
Sent to my son: nor leave t'admire the change
Of manners, and the breeding of our youth,
Within the kingdom, since myself was one.
When I was young, he lived not in the stews,   5
Durst have conceived a scorn, and uttered it,
On a grey head; age was authority
Against a buffoon: and a man had, then,
A certain reverence paid unto his years,
That had none due unto his life. So much   10

Scene [iii] Scene v in Ff
2 *admire* 'be surprised at'

---

84 *Higginbottom.* Not certainly identified—Stephen may mean Otwell
   Higgenbotham, a seditious disturber and a tenant of the Earl of Shrews-
   bury who had a notorious court dispute with him in 1579, in which the
   Queen interested herself. Stephen's meaning is clear: 'like any low
   fellow'. Beggars carried cudgels rather than swords.
5–7 *he . . . head.* 'Even a man who lived in a brothel would not have dared
   actually to *voice* contempt for his elders'. This passage is adapted from a
   part of Juvenal's Thirteenth Satire.
7–8 *age . . . buffoon.* This is elliptical: 'even a buffoon respected age'.

The sanctity of some prevailed, for others.
But, now, we all are fall'n; youth, from their fear:
And age, from that, which bred it, good example.
Nay, would ourselves were not the first, even parents,
That did destroy the hopes, in our own children: 15
Or they not learned our vices, in their cradles,
And sucked in our ill customs, with their milk.
Ere all their teeth be born, or they can speak,
We make their palates cunning! The first words,
We form their tongues with, are licentious jests!   20
Can it call, whore? Cry, bastard? Oh, then, kiss it,
A witty child! Can't swear? The father's dearling!
Give it two plums. Nay, rather than't shall learn
No bawdy song, the mother' herself will teach it!
But, this is in the infancy; the days   25
Of the long coat: when it puts on the breeches,
It will put off all this. Ay, it is like:
When it is gone into the bone already.
No, no: this dye goes deeper than the coat,
Or shirt, or skin. It stains, unto the liver,   30
And heart, in some. And, rather, than it should not,
Note, what we fathers do! Look, how we live!
What mistresses we keep! At what expense,
In our sons' eyes! Where they may handle our gifts,
Hear our lascivious courtships, see our dalliance,   35
Taste of the same provoking meats, with us,
To ruin of our states! Nay, when our own
Portion is fled, to prey on their remainder,
We call them into fellowship of vice!
Bait 'hem with the young chambermaid, to seal!   40

30 *liver* the seat of fleshly love
31 *heart* the seat of knowledge
36 *provoking meats* sexually stimulating food

12–34 This paraphrases Quintilian's *Institutes of Eloquence*: 'Would to
Heaven, that we ourselves were not the chief instruments in corrupting
the morals of our children . . . etc.'.

18–19 *Ere . . . cunning*. '. . . We pay more attention to his palate than his
pronunciation . . .' (Quintilian).

28–30 'This, at first, becomes habit, and habit grows into nature' (Quintilian).

37–40 *Nay . . . seal*. When the father has got through his own money, he
persuades his son to give up his rights to the estates (by offering him
the chambermaid), which he sells to maintain himself in his pro-
fligacy *seal* to seal the bargain; but a pun is involved on a figurative
sense of 'seal': 'to have sexual intercourse'; later this verb came to
mean 'impregnate'.

And teach 'hem all bad ways, to buy affliction!
This is one path! But there are millions more,
In which we spoil our own, with leading them.
Well, I thank heaven, I never yet was he,
That travelled with my son, before sixteen,   45
To show him, the Venetian courtesans.
Nor read the grammar of cheating, I had made
To my sharp boy, at twelve: repeating still
The rule, 'Get money'; still, 'get money, boy;
No matter by what means; money will do   50
More, boy, than my lord's letter'. Neither have I
Dressed snails, or mushrooms curiously before him,
Perfumed my sauces, and taught him to make 'hem;
Preceding still, with my grey gluttony,
At all the ordinaries: and only feared   55
His palate should degenerate, not his manners.
These are the trade of fathers, now! However
My son, I hope, hath met within my threshold,
None of these household precedents; which are strong,
And swift, to rape youth, to their precipice.   60
But, let the house at home be ne'er so clean—
Swept, or kept sweet from filth; nay, dust, and cobwebs:
If he will live, abroad, with his companions,
In dung, and leystalls; it is worth a fear.
Nor is the danger of conversing less,   65
Than all that I have mentioned of example.

            [*Enter*] BRAINWORM [*disguised as before*]

BRAINWORM
    [*Aside*] My master! Nay, faith have at you: I am fleshed
    now, I have sped so well.—Worshipful sir, I beseech you,
    respect the estate of a poor soldier; I am ashamed of this

41 *affliction* G+ affiction, F1 affection F2
55 *ordinaries* eating-houses
64 *leystalls* rubbish-heaps
67 *sped so well* been so fortunate

---

46 Venice was described in a contemporary play as 'the best flesh-shambles
    in Italy', and Venetian whores were accounted the best in Europe.
49 *still.* Ff prints the whole passage quoted here in italics; H & S correct
    this word, rightly I think, to Roman, but have been followed by no
    other editor.
50–60 *No matter . . . precipice.* There are two further adaptations from
    Juvenal's Fourteenth Satire in these lines.
67 *fleshed.* Encouraged (after his first successful encounter in disguise):
    hunting dogs who had been in at their first kill were said to be 'fleshed'.

base course of life—God's my comfort—but extremity   70
provokes me to't, what remedy?

KNO'WELL
I have not for you, now.

BRAINWORM
By the faith I bear unto truth, gentleman, it is no ordinary
custom in me, but only to preserve manhood. I protest to
you, a man I have been, a man I may be, by your sweet   75
bounty.

KNO'WELL
'Pray thee, good friend, be satisfied.

BRAINWORM
Good sir, by that hand, you may do the part of a kind
gentleman, in lending a poor soldier the price of two cans
of beer—a matter of small value. The king of heaven shall   80
pay you, and I shall rest thankful: sweet worship—

KNO'WELL
Nay, and you be so importunate—

BRAINWORM
Oh, tender sir, need will have his course: I was not made to
this vile use! Well, the edge of the enemy could not have
abated me so much: it's hard when a man hath served in his   85
prince's cause, and be thus—(*He weeps*) Honourable worship, let me derive a small piece of silver from you, it shall
not be given in the course of time, by this good ground, I
was fain to pawn my rapier last night for a poor supper, I had
sucked the hilts long before, I am a pagan else: sweet honour.   90

KNO'WELL
Believe me, I am taken with some wonder,
To think, a fellow of thy outward presence
Should, in the frame, and fashion of his mind,
Be so degenerate, and sordid-base!
Art thou a man? And sham'st thou not to beg?   95
To practise such a servile kind of life?
Why, were thy education ne'er so mean,
Having thy limbs, a thousand fairer courses
Offer themselves, to thy election.

79–80 *the price of two cans of beer* twopence

87–88 *it . . . time.* i.e. 'I'll pay it back'—Brainworm tries on a subtle
variation of the beggar's trick phrase 'God pays' ('cast your bread upon
the waters'): he implies that he will pay it back, but in sufficiently
ambiguous terms for him to be able to claim that he meant no more than
that Kno'well would be rewarded by God.

90 *hilts.* This formerly meant the protection of the handle, consisting of
two pieces; hence its later plural use to denote the handle.

Either the wars might still supply thy wants,   100
Or service of some virtuous gentleman,
Or honest labour: nay, what can I name,
But would become thee better than to beg?
But men of thy condition feed on sloth,
As doth the beetle, on the dung she breeds in,   105
Not caring how the mettle of your minds
Is eaten with the rust of idleness.
Now, afore me, whate'er he be, that should
Relieve a person of thy quality,
While thou insist'st in this loose desperate course,   110
I would esteem the sin, not thine, but his.

BRAINWORM

Faith sir, I would gladly find some other course, if so—

KNO'WELL

Ay, you'd gladly find it, but you will not seek it.

BRAINWORM

Alas sir, where should a man seek? In the wars, there's no
ascent by desert in these days, but—and for service, would   115
it were as soon purchased, as wished for. The air's my
comfort. [*Sighs*] I know, what I would say—

KNO'WELL

What's thy name?

BRAINWORM

                    Please you, Fitzsword, sir.

KNO'WELL   Fitzsword?

Say, that a man should entertain thee now,
Wouldst thou be honest, humble, just, and true?   120

BRAINWORM

Sir, by the place, and honour of a soldier—

KNO'WELL

Nay, nay, I like not these affected oaths;
Speak plainly man: what thinkst thou of my words?

BRAINWORM

Nothing, sir, but wish my fortunes were as happy, as my
service should be honest.   125

KNO'WELL

Well, follow me, I'll prove thee, if thy deeds
Will carry a proportion to thy words.

BRAINWORM

Yes sir, straight, I'll but garter my hose. [*Exit* KNO'WELL]
Oh that my belly were hooped now, for I am ready to burst
with laughing! Never was bottle, or bagpipe fuller. 'Slid,   130

116 *purchased* obtained
116–117 *The . . . comfort* 'all the comfort I get is air', i.e. nothing

was there ever seen a fox in years to betray himself thus?
Now shall I be possessed of all his counsels: and, by that
conduit, my young master. Well, he is resolved to prove my
honesty; faith, and I am resolved to prove his patience: Oh I
shall abuse him intolerably. This small piece of service,   135
will bring him clean out of love with the soldier, forever. He
will never come within the sign of it, the sight of a cassock,
or a musket-rest again. He will hate the musters at Mile End
for it, to his dying day. It's no matter, let the world think me
a bad counterfeit, if I cannot give him the slip, at an instant: 140
why, this is better than to have stayed his journey! Well,
I'll follow him: Oh, how I long to be employed.   [*Exit*]

Act III, Scene i

[*The Old Jewry. A Room in the Windmill Tavern*]

[*Enter*] MATTHEW, WELLBRED [*and*] BOBADILL

MATTHEW
Yes faith, sir, we were at your lodging to seek you, too.
WELLBRED
Oh, I came not there tonight.
BOBADILL
Your brother delivered us as much.
WELLBRED
Who? My brother Downright?
BOBADILL
He. Master Wellbred, I know not in what kind you hold me,   5
but let me say to you this: as sure as honour, I esteem it so
much out of the sunshine of reputation, to throw the least
beam of regard, upon such a—
WELLBRED
Sir, I must hear no ill words of my brother.

131 *in years* old
137 *cassock* used in its original sense: the loose outer coat worn by a
    soldier

---

131 *fox*. Brainworm feels himself justified in calling Kno'well a fox because
    of his scheme to follow his own son; this gives him supposedly moral
    grounds for cheating him.
138 *musket-rest*. Muskets were so clumsy until the invention of the fire-
    lock (not in general use in England until the Civil War) that they needed
    supports, which were carried by soldiers on their right shoulders.
    Mile End. Then a common often used as a training-ground.
140 *slip*. A counterfeit coin: a pun is involved between this sense and the
    familiar phrase.

BOBADILL

I, protest to you, as I have a thing to be saved about me, I   10
never saw any gentleman-like part—

WELLBRED

Good Captain, faces about, to some other discourse.

BOBADILL

With your leave, sir, and there were no more men living
upon the face of the earth, I should not fancy him, by St.
George.   15

MATTHEW

Troth, nor I, he is of a rustical cut, I know not how: he
doth not carry himself like a gentleman of fashion—

WELLBRED

Oh, Master Matthew, that's a grace peculiar but to a few;
quos aequus amavit Jupiter.

MATTHEW

I understand you sir.   20

WELLBRED

No question, you do, or you do not, sir.

          YOUNG KNO'WELL *enters* [*with* STEPHEN]

Ned Kno'well! By my soul welcome; how dost thou sweet
spirit, my genius. 'Slid I shall love Apollo, and the mad
Thespian girls the better, while I live, for this; my dear
fury: now, I see there's some love in thee! [*In a lower voice*]   25
Sirrah, these be the two I writ to thee of. Nay, what a drowsy
humour is this now? Why dost thou not speak?

ED. KNO'WELL

Oh, you are a fine gallant, you sent me a rare letter!

WELLBRED

Why, was't not rare?

ED. KNO'WELL

Yes, I'll be sworn, I was ne'er guilty of reading the like;   30
match it in all Pliny, or Symmachus's epistles, and I'll have
my judgement burned in the ear for a rogue: make much of

---

12 *faces about* a military term, perhaps not equivalent to 'wheel', as
    explained by G, but to 'about turn'

19 *quos . . . Jupiter.* Virgil, *Aeneid*, VI, 129–131: 'whom impartial Jupiter
    has loved'.

23–24 *Apollo . . . girls.* Apollo was the God of song, and the 'mad (i.e.
    poetically inspired) Thespian girls' are the nine Muses.

25 *fury.* Jocularly likens Ned to one of the Furies of Greek mythology.

31 *Symmachus' epistles.* A dull Fourth Century Roman consul who modelled
    his style on Pliny the Younger, the famous letter-writer of Trajan's age.

32 *judgement . . . rogue.* One of the punishments of rogues was branding
    on the ear.

thy vein, for it is inimitable. But I marle what camel it was,
that had the carriage of it, for doubtless, he was no ordinary
beast, that brought it!   35

WELLBRED
Why?

ED. KNO'WELL
Why, sayst thou? Why dost thou think that any reasonable
creature, especially in the morning—the sober time of the
day too—could have mista'en my father for me?

WELLBRED
'Slid, you jest, I hope?   40

ED. KNO'WELL
Indeed, the best use we can turn it to, is to make a jest on't,
now: but I'll assure you, my father had the full view o' your
flourishing style, some hour before I saw it.

WELLBRED
What a dull slave was this! But, sirrah, what said he to it, i'
faith?   45

ED. KNO'WELL
Nay, I know not what he said: but I have a shrewd guess
what he thought.

WELLBRED
What? What?

ED. KNO'WELL
Marry, that thou art some strange dissolute young fellow,
and I a grain or two better, for keeping thee company.   50

WELLBRED
Tut, that thought is like the moon in her last quarter, 'twill
change shortly: but sirrah, I pray thee be acquainted with
my two hang-byes here; thou wilt take exceeding pleasure
in 'hem if thou hear'st 'hem once go: my wind instruments.
I'll wind 'hem up—but what strange piece of silence is this?   55
The sign of the dumb man?

ED. KNO'WELL
Oh, sir, a kinsman of mine, one that may make your music
the fuller, and he please, he has his humour, sir.

33 *marle* marvel
    camel proverbially stupid
53 *hang-byes* contemptuous term for dependent or hanger-on
57 *your music* to be played on the 'wind instruments'

---

44 *What . . . this!* Refers to the servant who delivered the letter in I.i.
54–55 *wind-instruments . . . up.* Wind was pronounced as in the 'wind'
    of 'wind the clock'. Cf. *Hamlet* 3, ii.
56 *The . . . man.* While Stephen affects his fashionable melancholy,
    Wellbred compares him to an inn-sign.

WELLBRED

Oh, what is't? What is't?

ED. KNO'WELL

Nay, I'll neither do your judgement, nor his folly that   60
wrong, as to prepare your apprehension: I'll leave him to
the mercy o'your search, if you can take him, so.

WELLBRED

Well, Captain Bobadill, Master Matthew, pray you know this
gentleman here, he is a friend of mine, and one that will
deserve your affection. (*To* MASTER STEPHEN) I know not   65
your name sir, but I shall be glad of any occasion, to render
me more familiar to you.

STEPHEN

My name is Master Stephen, sir, I am this gentleman's own
cousin, sir, his father is mine uncle, sir, I am somewhat
melancholy, but you shall command me, sir, in whatsoever   70
is incident to a gentleman.

BOBADILL

(*To* [ED.] KNO'WELL) Sir, I must tell you this, I am no
general man, but for Master Wellbred's sake—you may
embrace it, at what height of favour you please—I do
communicate with you: and conceive you, to be a gentleman   75
of some parts, I love few words.

ED. KNO'WELL

And I fewer, sir. I have scarce enow, to thank you.

MATTHEW

(*To* MASTER STEPHEN) But are you indeed, sir? So given to it?

STEPHEN

Ay, truly, sir, I am mightily given to melancholy.

MATTHEW

Oh, it's only your fine humour, sir, your true melancholy   80
breeds your perfect fine wit, sir: I am melancholy myself
divers times, sir, and then do I no more but take pen, and
paper presently, and overflow you half a score, or a dozen
of sonnets, at a sitting.

ED. KNO'WELL

(*Aside*) Sure, he utters them then, by the gross.   85

---

62 *if you can take him, so* 'if you can work out what his humour is, so
   much the better'
73 *general* ordinary

80–83 *Oh . . . sir.* A criticism, put into Matthew's mouth, of the false,
   affected humour of melancholy (not of real melancholy).
85 *utters.* A contemptuous pun on the commercial sense of 'puts into
   circulation'.

STEPHEN

Truly sir, and I love such things, out of measure.

ED. KNO'WELL

I' faith, better than in measure, I'll undertake.

MATTHEW

Why, I pray you, sir, make use of my study, it's at your service.

STEPHEN

I thank you sir, I shall be bold, I warrant you; have you a   90
stool there, to be melancholy upon?

MATTHEW

That I have, sir, and some papers there of mine own doing, at idle hours, that you'll say there's some sparks of wit in 'hem, when you see them.

WELLBRED

[*Aside*] Would the sparks would kindle once, and become   95
a fire amongst 'hem, I might see self-love burnt for her heresy.

STEPHEN

Cousin, is it well? Am I melancholy enough?

ED. KNO'WELL

Oh ay, excellent!

WELLBRED

Captain Bobadill: why muse you so?

ED. KNO'WELL

He is melancholy, too.   100

BOBADILL

Faith, sir, I was thinking of a most honourable piece of service, was performed tomorrow, being St. Mark's day: shall be some ten years, now.

ED. KNO'WELL

In what place, Captain?

BOBADILL

Why, at the beleag'ring of Strigonium, where, in less than   105
two hours, seven hundred resolute gentlemen, as any were in Europe, lost their lives upon the breach. I'll tell you, gentlemen, it was the first, but the best leager, that ever I beheld, with these eyes, except the taking in of—what do you call it, last year, by the Genoways?—but that, of all other, was   110
the most fatal, and dangerous exploit, that ever I was ranged in, since I first bore arms before the face of the enemy, as I am a gentleman, and soldier.

---

108 *leager* siege   110 *Genoways* Genoese

86 *measure*. Stephen unconsciously puns on the sense of 'metre'.
105 *Strigonium*. Graan in Hungary, retaken from the Turks in 1595; it was fashionable (and unverifiable) to have fought against the Turks.

STEPHEN

'So, I had as lief, as an angel, I could swear as well as that
gentleman!   115

ED. KNO'WELL

Then, you were a servitor, at both it seems! At Strigonium?
And what-you-call't?

BOBADILL

Oh Lord, sir! By St. George, I was the first man, that
entered the breach: and, had I not effected it with resolution, I had been slain, if I had had a million of lives.   120

ED. KNO'WELL

'Twas pity, you had not ten; a cat's, and your own, i' faith.
But, was it possible?

MATTHEW

[*Aside to* STEPHEN] 'Pray you, mark this discourse, sir.

STEPHEN

[*To* MATTHEW] So, I do.

BOBADILL

I assure you, upon my reputation, 'tis true, and yourself shall   125
confess.

ED. KNO'WELL

You must bring me to the rack, first.

BOBADILL

Observe me judicially, sweet sir, they had planted me three
demi-culverins, just in the mouth of the breach; now, sir,
as we were to give on, their master-gunner—a man of no   130
mean skill, and mark, you must think—confronts me with
his linstock, ready to give fire; I spying his intendment,
discharged my petronel in his bosom, and with these single
arms, my poor rapier, ran violently, upon the Moors, that
guarded the ordnance, and put 'hem pell-mell to the sword.   135

WELLBRED

To the sword? To the rapier, Captain.

---

127 G+ add the s.d. *Aside* to this remark, but it seems
      hardly necessary, if uttered in a good-humoured way
129 *demi-culverins* nine-pounder cannon, of about 4½″ bore
130 *give on* attack
132 *linstock* a three-foot staff with a point at one end, to stick in the
      ground, and a forked head to hold a match (with which to fire a
      gun)
      intendment intention
133 *petronel* a large pistol

---

136 *rapier.* The more fashionable term: Wellbred parodies Bobadill's
      affected pedantry by satirical over-pedantry.

ED. KNO'WELL

Oh, it was a good figure observed, sir! But did you all this,
Captain, without hurting your blade?

BOBADILL

Without any impeach, o' the earth: you shall perceive sir.
[*Shows his rapier*] It is the most fortunate weapon, that ever   140
rid on gentleman's thigh: shall I tell you, sir? You talk of
Morglay, Excalibur, Durindana, or so? Tut, I lend no
credit to that is fabled of 'hem, I know the virtue of mine
own, and therefore I dare, the boldlier, maintain it.

STEPHEN

I marle whether it be a Toledo, or no?   145

BOBADILL

A most perfect Toledo, I assure you, sir.

STEPHEN

I have a countryman of his, here.

MATTHEW

Pray you, let's see, sir: yes faith, it is!

BOBADILL

This a Toledo? Pish.

STEPHEN

Why do you pish, Captain?   150

BOBADILL

A Fleming, by heaven, I'll buy them for a guilder, apiece,
an' I would have a thousand of them.

ED. KNO'WELL

How say you, cousin? I told you thus much.

WELLBRED

Where bought you it, Master Stephen?

STEPHEN

Of a scurvy rogue soldier—a hundred of lice go with him!   155
He swore it was a Toledo.

BOBADILL

A poor provant rapier, no better.

MATTHEW

Man, I think it be, indeed, now I look on't, better.

139 *impeach* injury; damage
151 *guilder* Dutch coin worth rather less than a florin
157 *provant* army issue, and therefore inferior

137 *figure.* Expression; but also 'metaphor', i.e. 'lie'. He means, 'Come
now, he told the lie with style!' innocuously smuggling in his real
opinion by means of the pun.
142 *Morglay, Excalibur, Durindana.* All famous swords of romance: of,
respectively, Bevis of 'Hamtown', King Arthur and Orlando (of
Orlando Furioso).

ED. KNO'WELL

Nay, the longer you look on't, the worse. Put it up, put it up.

STEPHEN

Well, I will put it up, but by— [*Aside*] I ha' forgot the   160
Captain's oath, I thought to ha' sworn by it—an' ere I meet
him—

WELLBRED

Oh, it is past help now, sir, you must have patience.

STEPHEN

Whoreson coney-catching rascal! I could eat the very hilts
for anger!   165

ED. KNO'WELL

A sign of good digestion! You have an ostrich stomach,
cousin.

STEPHEN

A stomach? Would I had him here, you should see, an' I had
a stomach.

WELLBRED

It's better as 'tis: come, gentlemen, shall we go?   170

[*Enter*] BRAINWORM [*disguised as before*]

ED. KNO'WELL

A miracle, cousin, look here! Look here!

STEPHEN

Oh, God's lid, by your leave, do you know me, sir?

BRAINWORM

Ay sir, I know you, by sight.

STEPHEN

You sold me a rapier, did you not?

BRAINWORM

Yes, marry, did I sir.   175

STEPHEN

You said, it was a Toledo, ha?

BRAINWORM

True, I did so.

STEPHEN

But, it is none?

171 begins Act III, Scene ii in Ff
172 *God's lid* G, Nn, Sh, H, S bowdlerize to "Od's lid', but F1 reads
    'gods lid'

164 *coney-catching*. Swindling: '. . . a name given to *deceivers*, by a
    metaphor taken from those that rob warrens . . .' (1617).
166 *ostrich stomach*. The ostrich is proverbial for its tough stomach, and is
    attracted by the brightness of metal, which it eats.
168 *stomach*. A pun on the figurative meaning of 'inclination', 'anger'.

BRAINWORM

No sir, I confess, it is none.

STEPHEN

Do you confess it? Gentlemen, bear witness, he has con-   180
fessed it. By God's will, and you had not confessed it—

ED. KNO'WELL

Oh cousin, forbear, forbear.

STEPHEN

Nay, I have done, cousin.

WELLBRED

Why, you have done like a gentleman, he has confessed it,
what would you more?   185

STEPHEN

Yes, by his leave, he is a rascal, under his favour, do you see?

ED. KNO'WELL

[*Aside to* WELLBRED] Ay, by his leave, he is, and under favour:
a pretty piece of civility! Sirrah, how dost thou like him?

WELLBRED

Oh, it's a most precious fool, make much on him: I can
compare him to nothing more happily, than a drum; for   190
everyone may play upon him.

ED. KNO'WELL

No, no, a child's whistle were far the fitter.

BRAINWORM

Sir, shall I entreat a word with you.   [*They move apart*]

ED. KNO'WELL

With me, sir? You have not another Toledo to sell, ha' you?

BRAINWORM

You are conceited, sir, your name is Master Kno'well, as I   195
take it?

ED. KNO'WELL

You are i' the right; you mean not to proceed in the cate-
chism, do you?

BRAINWORM

No sir, I am none of that coat.

ED. KNO'WELL

Of as bare a coat, though; well, say sir.   200

195 *conceited* witty, i.e. 'you're being funny'
199 *of that coat* i.e. not a curate
200 *of as bare a coat* i.e. as poor as a curate

186 *by his leave . . . under his favour.* Stephen, by the use of this formula,
    avoids the official necessity of being challenged to a duel.
191 *everyone may play upon.* Cf., again, *Hamlet* 3, ii.

BRAINWORM

Faith sir, I am but servant to the drum extraordinary, and
indeed, this smoky varnish being washed off, and three or
four patches removed, I appear your worship's in reversion,
after the decease of your good father, Brainworm.

ED. KNO'WELL

Brainworm! 'Slight, what breath of a conjurer, hath blown   205
thee hither in this shape?

BRAINWORM

The breath o' your letter, sir, this morning: the same that
blew you to the Windmill, and your father after you.

ED. KNO'WELL

My father?

BRAINWORM

Nay, never start, 'tis true, he has followed you over the   210
fields, by the foot, as you would do a hare i' the snow.

ED. KNO'WELL

Sirrah, Wellbred, what shall we do sirrah? My father is
come over, after me.

WELLBRED

Thy father? Where is he?

BRAINWORM

At Justice Clement's house here, in Coleman Street, where   215
he but stays my return; and then—

WELLBRED

Who's this? Brainworm?

BRAINWORM

The same, sir.

WELLBRED

Why how, i' the name of wit, com'st thou transmuted, thus?

BRAINWORM

Faith, a device, a device: nay, for the love of reason,   220
gentlemen, and avoiding the danger, stand not here, with-
draw, and I'll tell you all.

WELLBRED

But, art thou sure, he will stay thy return?

BRAINWORM

Do I live, sir? What a question is that?

WELLBRED

We'll prorogue his expectation then, a little: Brainworm,   225

201 *servant . . . extraordinary* 'I am only posing as a soldier'

215 *here.* F1, omitted in F2 and by G, Sh, N, H, S; but Coleman Street
    was a more obvious continuation of Old Jewry than it now is, and so
    might well have been regarded as the same street; moreover, at III.ii
    (F1) the scene may have shifted to the street.

thou shalt go with us. Come on, gentlemen, nay, I pray thee,
sweet Ned, droop not: 'heart, and our wits be so wretchedly
dull, that one old plodding brain can outstrip us all, would
we were e'en pressed, to make porters of; and serve out the
remnant of our days, in Thames Street, or at Custom House   230
quay, in a civil war, against the carmen.
BRAINWORM
Amen, amen, amen, say I.   [*Exeunt*]

Act III, Scene ii

[*The Old Jewry.* KITELY'S *Warehouse*]

[*Enter*] KITELY [*and*] CASH

KITELY
What says he, Thomas? Did you speak with him?
CASH
He says he will expect you, sir, within this half hour.
KITELY
Has he the money ready, can you tell?
CASH
Yes, sir, the money was brought in, last night.
KITELY
Oh, that's well: fetch me my cloak, my cloak.   [*Exit* CASH]   5
Stay, let me see, an hour, to go and come;
Ay, that will be the least: and then 'twill be
An hour, before I can dispatch with him;
Or very near: well, I will say two hours.
Two hours? Ha? Things, never dreamed of yet,   10
May be contrived, ay, and effected too,
In two hours' absence: well, I will not go.
Two hours; no, fleering opportunity,
I will not give your subtlety that scope.
Who will not judge him worthy to be robbed,   15
That sets his doors wide open to a thief,
And shows the felon, where his treasure lies?
Again, what earthy spirit but will attempt
To taste the fruit of beauty's golden tree,
When leaden sleep seals up the dragon's eyes?   20

   Scene [*ii*] Scene iii in Ff
13 *fleering* sneering; smiling obsequiously—a combination of these
   two meanings, both current in Jonson's time
19 *To taste . . . tree* see I.i, 185 n.

---

231 *carmen.* Carters: there was rivalry between the porters and the carmen,
   both of whom competed to transport goods.

I will not go. Business, go by, for once.
No, beauty, no; you are of too good caract,
To be left so, without a guard, or open!
Your lustre too'll inflame, at any distance,
Draw courtship to you, as a jet doth straws,   25
Put motion in a stone, strike fire from ice,
Nay, make a porter leap you, with his burden!
You must be then kept up, close, and well-watched,
For, give you opportunity, no quicksand
Devours, or swallows swifter! He that lends   30
His wife, if she be fair, or time, or place;
Compels her to be false. I will not go.
The dangers are too many. And, then, the dressing
Is a most main attractive! Our great heads,
Within the city, never were in safety,   35
Since our wives wore these little caps: I'll change 'hem,
I'll change 'hem, straight, in mine. Mine shall no more
Wear three-piled acorns, to make my horns ache.
Nor will I go. I am resolved for that.

              [*Enter* CASH, *with cloak*]

Carry' in my cloak again. Yet, stay. Yet, do too.   40
I will defer going, on all occasions.

CASH
    Sir. Snare, your scrivener, will be there with th' bonds.
KITELY
    That's true! Fool on me! I had clean forgot it,
    I must go. What's a clock?

22 *caract* carat
23 *open* Kitely's imagery is often highly sexual
34 *attractive* attraction
   great heads i.e. where cuckold's horns can easily be grown
36 *little caps* three-cornered velvet hats, fashionable among middle-
   class housewives

---

25 *jet.* Can magnetize by static electricity: this was one of the reasons for
   the popularity of jet rings.
27 *Nay . . . burden.* A striking line, suddenly shifting from the more or
   less delicate metaphors (though see 'open', above) of the preceding
   lines to a crude physical image: the play on 'burden' demonstrates
   Kitely's fascination with the idea of other men having sexual intercourse
   with (here, raping) his wife.
31 *place;* The semicolon at the end of this line is a good example of Jonson's
   use of it to convey an emphatic pause.
38 *three-piled acorns.* The 'little caps' referred to above *three-piled* of the
   best quality of velvet; a hart's head was called 'a velvet head' when its
   horns first appeared *my horns* cuckold's horns.

CASH　　　　　　　　　　　Exchange time, sir.

KITELY

[*Aside*] 'Heart, then will Wellbred presently be here, too,　45
With one, or other of his loose consorts.
I am a knave, if I know what to say,
What course to take, or which way to resolve.
My brain, methinks, is like an hour-glass,
Wherein, my' imaginations run, like sands,　　　　　　50
Filling up time; but then are turned, and turned:
So, that I know not what to stay upon,
And less, to put in act. It shall be so.
Nay, I dare build upon his secrecy,
He knows not to deceive.—Thomas!

CASH　　　　　　　　　　　Sir.　　　　　　55

KITELY

[*Aside*] Yet not, I have bethought me, too, I will not.—
Thomas, is Cob within?

CASH　　　　　　　　　I think he be, sir.

KITELY

[*Aside*] But he'll prate too, there's no speech of him.
No, there were no man o' the earth to Thomas,
If I durst trust him; there is all the doubt.　　　　　60
But, should he have a chink in him, I were gone,
Lost i' my fame for ever: talk for th' Exchange.
The manner he hath stood with, till this present,
Doth promise no such change! What should I fear then?
Well, come what will, I'll tempt my fortune, once.—　65
Thomas—you may deceive me, but, I hope—
Your love, to me, is more—

CASH　　　　　　　　　　Sir, if a servant's

Duty, with faith, may be called love, you are
More than in hope, you are possessed of it.

KITELY

I thank you, heartily, Thomas; gi' me your hand:　70
With all my heart, Good Thomas. I have, Thomas,

---

59 *to* compared to
68 *Duty* duetie F1

---

44 *Exchange time*. 'Past ten' in Q; some authorities give ten as the opening
hour for business on the Exchange, others eleven.

61 *chink*. A crack in a container; the Q reading 'if he should prove,
Rimarum plenus' (full of chinks; leaky) throws light on this. Jonson
must have known Terence's *Eunuch*, in which a servant, Parmeno,
says that he can keep a secret if it is true, but that if it is false, he is
'full of leaks' ('plenus rimarum sum'). In other words, Kitely's reluct-
ance to impart this information is based 1. on his awareness of its
falsity, 2. on his guilty half-knowledge of his hidden motives.

A secret to impart, unto you—but
When once you have it, I must seal your lips up:
So far, I tell you, Thomas.

CASH   Sir, for that—

KITELY
Nay, hear me, out. Think, I esteem you, Thomas,   75
When, I will let you in, thus, to my private.
It is a thing sits, nearer, to my crest,
Than thou art ware of, Thomas. If thou should'st
Reveal it, but—

CASH   How? I reveal it?

KITELY   Nay,
I do not think thou would'st; but if thou should'st: 80
'Twere a great weakness.

CASH   A great treachery.
Give it no other name.

KITELY   Thou wilt not do't, then?

CASH
Sir, if I do, mankind disclaim me, ever.

KITELY
[Aside] He will not swear, he has some reservation,
Some concealed purpose, and close meaning, sure: 85
Else, being urged so much, how should he choose,
But lend an oath to all this protestation?
He's no precisian, that I am certain of.
Nor rigid Roman Catholic. He'll play,
At fayles, and tick-tack, I have heard him swear.   90
What should I think of it? Urge him again,
And by some other say? I will do so.—
Well, Thomas, thou hast sworn not to disclose;
Yes, you did swear?

CASH   Not yet, sir, but I will,
Please you—

74 *So . . . Thomas* (So . . . Thomas), Ff
88 *precisian* puritan
90 *fayles* a kind of backgammon
   tick-tack or tric-trac, another variety of backgammon

---

76 *private.* Privacy; but a hidden pun is involved, on 'private parts',
   especially in view of the pun in the next line; Q, significantly, reads 'my
   private thoughts'.
77 *crest.* A quadruple pun: 1. honour, 2. family, 3. cuckold's horns, 4. erect
   penis (i.e. 'what excites me sexually').
90 *swear.* A subtle and revealing pun, referring to 'swear' in both the sense
   of 'make oaths' and 'take an oath': it serves to show how little Kitely's
   anxiety about Cash is really affecting him—he might as well have
   sworn for all it matters. See ll. 101–102 below, 'It's . . . rock'.

KITELY
  No, Thomas, I dare take thy word.   95
  But; if thou wilt swear, do, as thou think'st good;
  I am resolved without it; at thy pleasure.
CASH
  By my soul's safety then, sir, I protest.
  My tongue shall ne'er take knowledge of a word,
  Delivered me in nature of your trust.   100
KITELY
  It's too much, these ceremonies need not,
  I know thy faith to be as firm as rock.
  Thomas, come hither, near: we cannot be
  Too private, in this business. So it is—
  [*Aside*] Now, he has sworn, I dare the safelier venture—   105
  I have of late, by divers observations—
  [*Aside*] But whether his oath can bind him, yea, or no;
  Being not taken lawfully? Ha? Say you?
  I will ask counsel, ere I do proceed—
  Thomas, it will be now too late to stay,   110
  I'll spy some fitter time soon, or tomorrow.
CASH
  Sir, at your pleasure?
KITELY   I will think. And, Thomas,
  I pray you search the books 'gainst my return,
  For the receipts 'twixt me, and Traps.
CASH   I will, sir.
KITELY
  And, hear you, if your mistress' brother, Wellbred,   115
  Chance to bring hither any gentlemen,
  Ere I come back; let one straight bring me word.
CASH
  Very well, sir.
KITELY   To the Exchange; do you hear?
  Or here in Coleman Street, to Justice Clement's.
  Forget it not, nor be not out of the way.   120
CASH
  I will not, sir.
KITELY   I pray you have a care on't.
  Or whether he come, or no, if any other,
  Stranger, or else, fail not to send me word.
CASH
  I shall not, sir.

---

119 *here*. See III.i, 215 n. This is retained, inconsistently, by G, Sh, N, H,
    S: Kitely's warehouse is in Old Jewry.
    Begins Act III Scene iv in Ff.

KITELY   Be't your special business
  Now, to remember it.
CASH   Sir. I warrant you.   125
KITELY
  But, Thomas, this is not the secret, Thomas,
  I told you of.
CASH   No, sir. I do suppose it.
KITELY
  Believe me, it is not.
CASH   Sir. I do believe you.
KITELY
  By heaven, it is not, that's enough. But, Thomas,
  I would not, you should utter it, do you see?   130
  To any creature living, yet, I care not.
  Well, I must hence. Thomas, conceive this much.
  It was a trial of you, when I meant
  So deep a secret to you, I mean not this,
  But that I have to tell you, this is nothing, this.   135
  But, Thomas, keep this from my wife, I charge you,
  Locked up in silence, midnight, buried here.
  [*Aside*] No greater hell, than to be slave to fear.   [*Exit*]
CASH
  'Locked up in silence, midnight, buried here'.
  Whence should this flood of passion, trow, take head? Ha?   140
  Best, dream no longer of this running humour,
  For fear I sink! The violence of the stream
  Already hath transported me so far,
  That I can feel no ground at all! But soft,
  Oh, 'tis our water-bearer: somewhat has crossed him, now.   145

[Enter] COB

COB
  Fasting days? What would you tell me of fasting days? 'Slid,
  would they were all on a light fire for me: they say, the whole
  world shall be consumed with fire one day, but would I had

---

147 *on a light fire* ablaze

---

146 *Fasting days.* A very unpopular relic of pre-Reformation days, adhered
    to by the Government for economic rather than religious reasons; the
    Government claimed that this helped the English fishing industry, and
    they put a heavy imposition on imported fish. In fact the English
    fishing industry was inefficient because of a shortage of fishing vessels,
    and foreign competitors could not be kept out of London. This speech
    of Cob's against 'Cecil's fast', as they called it, would certainly have
    drawn applause from the audience.

these ember-weeks, and villainous Fridays burnt, in the
meantime, and then—   150

CASH

Why, how now Cob, what moves thee to this choler? Ha?

COB

Collar, Master Thomas? I scorn your collar, ay sir, I am
none o' your cart-horse, though I carry, and draw water.
An' you offer to ride me, with your collar, or halter either, I
may hap show you a jade's trick, sir.   155

CASH

Oh, you'll slip your head out of the collar? Why, goodman
Cob, you mistake me.

COB

Nay, I have my rheum, and I can be angry as well as another,
sir.

CASH

Thy rheum, Cob? Thy humour, thy humour? Thou mis-   160
tak'st.

COB

Humour? Mack, I think it be so, indeed: what is that
humour? Some rare thing, I warrant.

CASH

Marry, I'll tell thee, Cob: it is a gentleman-like monster,
bred, in the special gallantry of our time, by affectation; and   165
fed by folly.

COB

How? Must it be fed?

CASH

Oh ay, humour is nothing, if it be not fed. Didst thou never
hear that? It's a common phrase, 'Feed my humour'.

COB

I'll none on it: humour, avaunt, I know you not, begone.   170
Let who will make hungry meals for your monstership, it
shall not be I. Feed you, quoth he? 'Slid, I ha' much ado, to
feed myself; especially, on these lean rascally days, too; and't
had been any other day, but a fasting day—a plague on
them all for me—by this light, one might have done the   175
commonwealth good service, and have drowned them all i'

149 *ember-weeks* regular periods when priests were prepared for
ordination
162 *Mack* a corruption of 'mass'

---

158 *rheum*. The term 'humour' had superseded this: Cob is hopelessly old-
fashioned.
169 *'Feed my humour.'* This phrase is found in several works, including
Lyly's *Euphues and his England* (1580).

the flood, two or three hundred thousand years ago. Oh, I do
stomach them hugely! I have a maw now, and 'twere for Sir
Bevis his horse, against 'hem.

CASH

I pray thee, good Cob, what makes thee so out of love with   180
fasting days?

COB

Marry that, which will make any man out of love with 'hem,
I think: their bad conditions, and you will needs know.
First, they are of a Flemish breed, I am sure on't, for they
ravin up more butter, than all the days of the week, beside;   185
next, they stink of fish, and leek-porridge miserably: thirdly,
they'll keep a man devoutly hungry, all day, and at night
send him supperless to bed.

CASH

Indeed, these are faults, Cob.

COB

Nay, and this were all, 'twere something, but they are the   190
only known enemies, to my generation. A fasting day, no
sooner comes, but my lineage goes to rack, poor cobs they
smoke for it, they are made martyrs o' the gridiron, they
melt in passion: and your maids too know this, and yet
would have me turn Hannibal, and eat my own fish, and   195
blood: my princely coz (*He pulls out a red herring*), fear
nothing; I have not the heart to devour you, and I might be
made as rich as King Cophetua. Oh, that I had room for my
tears, I could weep salt water enough, now, to preserve the
lives of ten thousand of my kin. But I may curse none but   200
these filthy Almanacs, for an'twere not for them, these days
of persecution would ne'er be known. I'll be hanged, an'

178 *stomach* loathe
    maw hunger
185 *ravin* devour
195 *Hannibal* a malapropism for 'cannibal'

178–179 *Sir Bevis his horse.* Sir Bevis of 'Hamtown's' famous war-horse,
    Arundel. Cob either means that he is imbued with Arundel's celebrated
    pugnacity or, more likely, that he is angry enough to eat Arundel to
    demonstrate his wrath against fasting days (this being, say H & S, 'his
    notion of hyperbole').
184–185 *Flemish . . . butter.* The Dutch were proverbially keen on butter.
195 *fish.* The compositor of the relevant passage in F3 humourlessly sub-
    stituted 'flesh', and has been followed, somewhat amazingly, by G,
    Sh, N, H, S.
198 *Cophetua.* African King more famous for his marriage to the beggar-
    maid Penelophon (there was a ballad on the subject) than for his wealth;
    S suggests Cob may have been thinking of Croesus.

some fishmonger's son do not make of 'hem; and puts in
more fasting days than he should do, because he would utter
his father's dried stock-fish, and stinking conger.   205

CASH
'Slight, peace, thou'lt be beaten like a stock-fish, else: here
is Master Matthew. Now must I look out for a messenger to
my master.   [*Exit with* COB]

[*Enter*] WELLBRED, ED. KNO'WELL, BRAINWORM,
BOBADILL, MATTHEW [*and*] STEPHEN

WELLBRED
Beshrew me, but it was an absolute good jest, and exceed-
ingly well carried!   210
ED. KNO'WELL
Ay, and our ignorance maintained it as well, did it not?
WELLBRED
Yes faith, but was't possible thou should'st not know him?
I forgive Master Stephen, for he is stupidity itself!
ED. KNO'WELL
'Fore God, not I, and I might have been joined patten with
one of the seven wise masters, for knowing him. He had so   215
writhen himself, into the habit of one of your poor infantry,
your decayed, ruinous, worm-eaten gentlemen of the round:
such as have vowed to sit on the skirts of the city, let your

204 *utter* put into public circulation
209 Begins III.v in Ff
     but it was i.e. 'if it wasn't'
216 *writhen* contorted
218 *sit on the skirts of the city* make themselves a nuisance in the city

---

203 *fishmonger's son.* The fishmongers were always ready to help the
     authorities to discover people who sold meat on Fridays.
206 *beaten like a stock-fish.* Dried cod was so heavily salted that it had to be
     beaten before it was boiled.
214–228 *'Fore God . . . regiment.* This and Ed. Kno'well's next speech are
     almost certainly a tribute to the acting of Burbage as Brainworm.
214 *joined patten.* Shared in an office or privilege by letters-patent; probably
     young Kno'well means 'Even I couldn't have recognized Brainworm
     unless I had shared a monopoly of wisdom with one of the seven wise
     masters' (these were Bias, Pittacus, Cleobulus, Periander, Solon,
     Chilon and Thales).
217 *gentlemen of the round.* These were soldiers of inferior rank, although
     superior in station to the common man, who 'went the rounds', i.e.
     did sentry-go, of a military camp. Here young Kno'well means beggars
     of the type Brainworm has been impersonating. Q has 'disparviews',
     poor beggars, instead of 'infantry'.

provost, and his half-dozen of halbadiers do what they can;
and have translated begging out of the old hackney pace, to   220
a fine easy amble, and made it run as smooth, off the tongue,
as a shove-groat shilling. Into the likeness of one of these
reformados had he moulded himself so perfectly, observing
every trick of their action, as varying the accent, swearing
with an emphasis, indeed all, with so special, and exquisite   225
a grace, that—hadst thou seen him—thou wouldst have
sworn, he might have been sergeant-major, if not lieutenant-
colonel to the regiment.

WELLBRED
Why, Brainworm, who would have thought thou hadst been
such an artificer?   230

ED. KNO'WELL
An artificer! An architect! Except a man had studied
begging all his lifetime, and been a weaver of language, from
his infancy, for the clothing of it! I never saw his rival.

WELLBRED
Where got'st thou this coat, I marle?

BRAINWORM
Of a Houndsditch man, sir. One of the devil's near kinsmen,   235
a broker.

WELLBRED
That cannot be, if the proverb hold; for, a crafty knave needs
no broker.

BRAINWORM
True sir, but I did need a broker, ergo.

WELLBRED
Well put off—no crafty knave, you'll say.   240

---

219 *provost* officer-in-charge of discipline
   halbadiers members of a civic guard who carried a halberd as
      badge of office
220 *hackney pace* slow; cf. the proverb 'To go upon the Fran-
      ciscan's hackney'—i.e. by foot
222 *shove-groat shilling* smooth shilling used in shovel-board, which
      was similar to shove-halfpenny
223 *reformados* disbanded soldiers (owing to the re-forming of their
      companies)
227 *sergeant-major* then a commissioned officer immediately below
      lieutenant-colonel in rank; a cross between a modern major and
      an adjutant
230 *artificer* artist
232 *weaver of language* romancer; liar
235 *Houndsditch* famous for its (devilish) brokers and its clothiers
239 *ergo* therefore

ED. KNO'WELL
Tut, he has more of these shifts.
BRAINWORM
And yet where I have one, the broker has ten, sir.

[*Enter*] CASH

CASH
Francis, Martin, ne'er a one to be found, now? What a
spite's this?
WELLBRED
How now, Thomas? Is my brother Kitely, within?   245
CASH
No sir, my master went forth e'en now: but Master Down-
right is within. Cob, what Cob! Is he gone too?
WELLBRED
Whither went your master? Thomas, canst thou tell?
CASH
I know not, to Justice Clement's, I think, sir. Cob!
                                              [*Exit* CASH]
ED. KNO'WELL
Justice Clement, what's he?   250
WELLBRED
Why, dost thou not know him? He is a city magistrate, a
justice here, an excellent good lawyer, and a great scholar:
but the only mad, merry, old fellow in Europe! I showed
him you, the other day.
ED. KNO'WELL
Oh, is that he? I remember him now. Good faith, and he has 255
a very strange presence, methinks; it shows as if he stood
out of the rank, from other men: I have heard many of his jests
i' the university. They say, he will commit a man, for taking
the wall, of his horse.
WELLBRED
Ay, or wearing his cloak of one shoulder, or serving of God: 260
anything indeed, if it come in the way of his humour.

243 *Francis, Martin* names of Kitely's servants
258 *i' the university* i' university', F1
260 *of one shoulder* on

---

241 *shifts*. 1. devices, 2. shirts. Brainworm plays on the second meaning in
    his retort.
258–259 *taking the wall, of his horse*. To take the wall was to walk in the
    drier part of the street (i.e. by the wall): the suggestion here is that
    Clement is so 'out of the rank from other men' as to commit anyone
    who did not give the dry side (as one did automatically to superiors) to
    his horse.

CASH *goes in and out calling*

CASH
Gasper, Martin, Cob! 'Heart, where should they be, trow?

BOBADILL
Master Kitely's man, 'pray thee vouchsafe us the lighting
of this match.

CASH
Fire on your match, no time but now to vouchsafe? Francis,   265
Cob!

BOBADILL
Body of me! Here's the remainder of seven pound, since
yesterday was seven-night. 'Tis your right Trinidado! Did
you never take any, Master Stephen?

STEPHEN
No truly, sir: but I'll learn to take it now, since you com-   270
mend it, so.

BOBADILL
Sir, believe me, upon my relation, for what I tell you, the
world shall not reprove. I have been in the Indies, where this
herb grows, where neither myself, nor a dozen gentlemen
before, of my knowledge, have received the taste of any   275
other nutriment, in the world, for the space of one and
twenty weeks, but the fume of this simple only. Therefore,
it cannot be, but 'tis most divine! Further, take it in the
nature, in the true kind so, it makes an antidote, that, had
you taken the most deadly poisonous plant in all Italy, it   280
should expel it, and clarify you, with as much ease, as I speak.
And, for your green wound, your Balsamum, and your St.
John's wort are all mere gulleries, and trash to it, especially
your Trinidado: your Nicotian is good too. I could say what
I know of the virtue of it, for the expulsion of rheums, raw   285
humours, crudities, obstructions, with a thousand of this
kind; but I profess myself no quacksalver. Only, thus much,
by Hercules, I do hold it, and will affirm it, before any prince
in Europe, to be the most sovereign, and precious weed, that
ever the earth tendered to the use of man.   290

265 *Fire* i.e. 'to hell with': Q reads 'A pox on'
268 *Trinidado* supposed to be the finest tobacco
278 *divine* a stock epithet
282 *green wound* raw, open wound (which Balsamum was supposed to
   'glue together')
284 *Nicotian* a comic blunder: one might now say: 'the West Indian
   plant is best, but nicotine's very good, too'

272–290 A satire on the affected praises of tobacco that were then current.

ED. KNO'WELL

This speech would ha' done decently in a tobacco-trader's mouth!

[*Enter* CASH *with* COB]

CASH

At Justice Clement's, he is: in the middle of Coleman Street.

COB

Oh, oh!

BOBADILL

Where's the match I gave thee? Master Kitely's man?   295

CASH

Would his match, and he, and pipe, and all were at Santo
Domingo! I had forgot it.   [*Exit*]

COB

By God's me, I marle, what pleasure, or felicity they have
in taking this roguish tobacco! It's good for nothing, but to
choke a man, and fill him full of smoke, and embers: there   300
were four died out of one house, last week, with taking of it,
and two more the bell went for, yesternight; one of them,
they say, will ne'er scape it: he voided a bushel of soot
yesterday, upward, and downward. By the stocks, an' there
were no wiser men than I, I'd have it present whipping,   305
man, or woman, that should but deal with a tobacco-pipe;
why, it will stifle them all in the end, as many as use it; it's
little better than ratsbane, or rosaker.

BOBADILL *beats* [COB] *with a cudgel*

ALL

Oh, good Captain, hold, hold.

BOBADILL

You base cullion, you.   310

[*Enter* CASH]

291 *decently* fittingly
294 *Oh, oh!* Cash has him by the ear
296–297 *Santo Domingo* famous for tobacco
308 *ratsbane, or rosaker* both preparations of arsenic
310 *cullion* originally 'testicle', hence 'vile fellow'

291 *tobacco-trader's.* Q reads 'pothecaries': by the time Jonson came to
revise the play tobacco-selling had passed from being an apothecary's
sideline, and had become a separate business.
301 *four died.* Such tales were current, with lurid details, such as that 'their
dead bodies being opened, had all their entrails as black as a coal, and
the very fat in their bodies resembling . . . rusty, or reesed bacon'
(1616). Similar foolish dicta are to be found in James I's *A Counter-
blast to Tobacco* (1604).

CASH

Sir, here's your match: come, thou must needs be talking,
too, thou'rt well enough served.

COB

Nay, he will not meddle with his match, I warrant you: well
it shall be a dear beating, and I live.

BOBADILL

Do you prate? Do you murmur?   315

ED. KNO'WELL

Nay, good Captain, will you regard the humour of a fool?
Away, knave.

WELLBRED

Thomas, get him away.   [*Exit* CASH *with* COB]

BOBADILL

A whoreson filthy slave, a dung-worm, an excrement! Body
o' Caesar, but that I scorn to let forth so mean a spirit, I'd   320
ha' stabbed him, to the earth.

WELLBRED

Marry, the law forbid, sir.

BOBADILL

By Pharaoh's foot, I would have done it.

STEPHEN

[*Aside*] Oh, he swears admirably! By Pharaoh's foot! Body o'
Caesar! I shall never do it, sure, upon mine honour, and by   325
St. George, no, I ha' not the right grace.

MATTHEW

Master Stephen, will you any? By this air, the most divine
tobacco, that ever I drunk!

STEPHEN

None, I thank you, sir. Oh, this gentleman does it, rarely
too! But nothing like the other. (MASTER STEPHEN *is prac-*   330
tising, to the post) By this air, as I am a gentleman: by—

BRAINWORM

[*Pointing at* STEPHEN] Master, glance, glance! Master Wellbred!
                                [*Exeunt* BOBADILL *and* MATTHEW]

313–314 *Nay ... live.* These are prophetic words, in view of Downright's
    later treatment of Bobadill *meddle with his match* 'meddle with your
    match' was a proverbial saying, meaning by implication, 'don't be a
    bully: take on someone of your own capacity', here quibbled upon.
328 *drunk.* Applied to tobacco as well as to alcohol, owing to a pun on 'pipe'.
    H & S quote 'Wine, you and I come both out of a pipe' (1630).
330–331 s.d. These posts were in Finsbury Fields, so Stephen must be
    imagining that one is in front of him.

STEPHEN

As I have somewhat to be saved, I protest—

WELLBRED

You are a fool: it needs no affidavit.

ED. KNO'WELL

Cousin, will you any tobacco?   335

STEPHEN

I sir! Upon my reputation—

ED. KNO'WELL

How now, cousin!

STEPHEN

I protest, as I am a gentleman, but no soldier, indeed—

WELLBRED

No, Master Stephen? As I remember your name is entered
in the Artillery Garden?   340

STEPHEN

Ay sir, that's true: cousin, may I swear, as I am a soldier,
by that?

ED. KNO'WELL

Oh yes, that you may. It's all you have for your money.

STEPHEN

Then, as I am a gentleman, and a soldier, it is divine
tobacco!   345

WELLBRED

But soft, where's Master Matthew? Gone?

BRAINWORM

No, sir, they went in here.

WELLBRED

Oh, let's follow them: Master Matthew is gone to salute his
mistress, in verse. We shall ha' the happiness, to hear some
of his poetry, now. He never comes unfurnished. Brainworm?   350

STEPHEN

Brainworm? Where? Is this Brainworm?

ED. KNO'WELL

Ay, cousin, no words of it, upon your gentility.

---

333 *As . . . protest.* Stephen's remarks consist of a series of vacuous affec-
    tations; he is continually attempting to imitate Bobadill.
339–340 *your name . . . Garden.* The Artillery Garden was in Bishopsgate;
    Stephen must have been a member of the Honourable Artillery Com-
    pany, a kind of Territorial body, not taken by Jonson, in his other
    allusions to it, with the utmost seriousness.
350 *He . . . unfurnished.* A phenomenon associated with bad poets that has
    not vanished with the passage of time.

STEPHEN
Not I, body of me, by this air, St. George, and the foot of
Pharaoh.
WELLBRED
Rare! Your cousin's discourse is simply drawn out with   355
oaths.
ED. KNO'WELL
'Tis larded with 'hem. A kind of French dressing, if you
love it.   [*Exeunt*]

Act III, Scene [iii]

[*Coleman Street. A Room in* JUSTICE CLEMENT'S *House*]

[*Enter*] KITELY [*and*] COB

KITELY
Ha? How many are there, sayest thou?
COB
Marry sir, your brother, Master Wellbred.
KITELY
Tut, beside him: what strangers are there, man?
COB
Strangers? Let me see, one, two; mass I know not well,
there are so many.   5
KITELY
How? So many?
COB
Ay, there's some five, or six of them, at the most.
KITELY
[*Aside*] A swarm, a swarm,
Spite of the devil, how they sting my head
With forked stings, thus wide, and large!—But, Cob,   10
How long hast thou been coming hither, Cob?

357 *larded* garnished

353–354 *Not . . . Pharaoh.* All editors (except H & S) supply exclamation
marks after each of Stephen's oaths, but this shows insensitivity to
Jonson's intentions: when at last he does have the opportunity to reel
out an impressive string of oaths, he does so mechanically and un-
emphatically—hence Wellbred's sarcastic retort.
357 *French dressing.* The French were famous for their skill in garnishing
meat, and for their elegant profanity, which was much copied by the
English.
Scene [iii] Scene vi in Ff
10 *forked stings.* Once again Kitely works in a reference to the cuckold's
horns.

COB
A little while, sir.
KITELY   Didst thou come running?
COB   No, sir.
KITELY
[*Aside*] Nay, then I am familiar with thy haste!
Bane to my fortunes: what meant I to marry?
I, that before was ranked in such content,   15
My mind at rest too, in so soft a peace,
Being free master of mine own free thoughts,
And now become a slave? What? Never sigh,
Be of good cheer, man: for thou art a cuckold,
'Tis done, 'tis done! Nay, when such flowing store,   20
Plenty itself, falls in my wife's lap,
The cornucopiae will be mine, I know.—But, Cob,
What entertainment had they? I am sure
My sister, and my wife, would bid them welcome! Ha?
COB
Like enough, sir, yet, I heard not a word of it.   25
KITELY
No: their lips were sealed with kisses, and the voice
Drowned in a flood of joy, at their arrival,
Had lost her motion, state, and faculty.
Cob, which of them was't, that first kissed my wife?
My sister, I should say. My wife, alas,   30
I fear not her: ha? Who was it, say'st thou?
COB
By my troth, sir, will you have the truth of it?
KITELY
Oh ay, good Cob: I pray thee, heartily.
COB
Then, I am a vagabond, and fitter for Bridewell, than your
worship's company, if I saw anybody to be kissed, unless   35
they would have kissed the post, in the middle of the ware-
house; for there I left them all, at their tobacco, with a pox.

34 *Bridewell* a workhouse
36 *kissed the post* 'to kiss the post' was a proverbial saying meaning
'to be shut out (from a meal)' as a consequence of being too late

22 *cornucopiae.* This is the etymologically correct form of 'Cornucopia',
   the horn of plenty; Kitely again puns on the sense of cuckold's horns,
   and characteristically relates the image of his cuckolding to a graphically
   sexual picture of it falling in his 'wife's lap'; it is interesting that he
   regards the 'threat' to his peace as being in fact a 'flowing store', a
   cornucopia—both images associated with good rather than bad things.

KITELY

How? Were they not gone in, then, ere thou cam'st?

COB

Oh no sir.

KITELY

Spite of the devil! What do I stay here, then? Cob, follow me.   40

[*Exit*]

COB

Nay, soft and fair, I have eggs on the spit; I cannot go yet,
sir. Now am I for some five and fifty reasons hammering,
hammering revenge: oh, for three or four gallons of vinegar,
to sharpen my wits. Revenge: vinegar revenge: vinegar, and
mustard revenge: nay, and he had not lien in my house,   45
'twould never have grieved me, but being my guest, one,
that I'll be sworn, my wife has lent him her smock off her
back, while his one shirt has been at washing; pawned her
neckerchers for clean bands for him; sold almost all my
platters, to buy him tobacco; and he to turn monster of   50
ingratitude, and strike his lawful host! Well, I hope to raise
up an host of fury for't: here comes Justice Clement.

[*Enter*] CLEMENT, KNO'WELL *and* FORMAL

CLEMENT

What's Master Kitely gone? Roger?

FORMAL

Ay, sir.

CLEMENT

'Heart o' me! What made him leave us so abruptly?—How   55
now, sirrah? What make you here? What would you have,
ha?

COB

And't please your worship, I am a poor neighbour of your
worship's—

CLEMENT

A poor neighbour of mine? Why, speak poor neighbour.   60

COB

I dwell, sir, at the sign of the Water-tankard, hard by the

45 *lien* past participle of 'lie'
49 *neckerchers* a kerchief worn round the neck
   bands a ruff or collar worn round the neck
53 begins Act III, Scene vii in Ff

---

41 *I have eggs on the spit*. 'I am very busy'; this seems to be the first
   appearance of this proverbial saying in print.
44-45 *Revenge . . . mustard revenge* a comic parody of the Revenge rant
   in *The Spanish Tragedy*.

Green Lattice: I have paid scot, and lot there, any time this
eighteen years.

CLEMENT

To the Green Lattice?

COB

No, sir, to the parish: marry, I have seldom scaped scot-free,   65
at the Lattice.

CLEMENT

Oh, well! What business has my poor neighbour with me?

COB

And't like your worship, I am come, to crave the peace of
your worship.

CLEMENT

Of me knave? Peace of me, knave? Did I e'er hurt thee? Or   70
threaten thee? Or wrong thee? Ha?

COB

No, sir, but your worship's warrant, for one that has
wronged me, sir: his arms are at too much liberty, I would
fain have them bound to a treaty of peace, an' my credit
could compass it, with your worship.   75

CLEMENT

Thou goest far enough about for't, I'm sure.

KNO'WELL

Why, dost thou go in danger of thy life for him? Friend?

COB

No sir; but I go in danger of my death, every hour, by his
means: an' I die, within a twelve-month and a day, I may
swear, by the law of the land, that he killed me.   80

CLEMENT

How? How knave? Swear he killed thee? And by the law?
What pretence? What colour hast thou for that?

COB

Marry, and't please your worship, both black, and blue;
colour enough, I warrant you. I have it here, to show your
worship.   [*Shows his bruises*]   85

CLEMENT

What is he, that gave you this, sirrah?

COB

A gentleman, and a soldier, he says he is, o' the city here.

CLEMENT

A soldier o' the city? What call you him?

62 *the Green Lattice*. Lattices (usually painted red) were put up outside
most inns, so that passers-by could not clearly discern what was going
on inside.
   scot, and lot. Elizabethan equivalent of rates; a parish assessment.
79–80 *within . . . me*. Cob's law is correct.

COB

Captain Bobadill.

CLEMENT

Bobadill? And why did he bob, and beat you, sirrah? How   90
began the quarrel betwixt you: ha? Speak truly knave, I
advise you.

COB

Marry, indeed, and please your worship, only because I
spake against their vagrant tobacco, as I came by 'hem, when
they were taking on't, for nothing else.   95

CLEMENT

Ha? You speak against tobacco? Formal, his name.

FORMAL

What's your name, sirrah?

COB

Oliver, sir, Oliver Cob, sir.

CLEMENT

Tell Oliver Cob, he shall go to the jail, Formal.

FORMAL

Oliver Cob, my master, Justice Clement, says, you shall go 100
to the jail.

COB

Oh, I beseech your worship, for God's sake, dear Master
Justice.

CLEMENT

Nay, God's precious: and such drunkards, and tankards, as
you are, come to dispute of tobacco once; I have done!   105
Away with him.

COB

Oh, good Master Justice, sweet old gentleman.

KNO'WELL

Sweet Oliver, would I could do thee any good: Justice
Clement, let me entreat you, sir.

CLEMENT

What? A threadbare rascal! A beggar! A slave that never   110
drunk out of better than pisspot metal in his life! And he to
deprave, and abuse the virtue of an herb, so generally
received in the courts of princes, the chambers of nobles,

---

  90 *bob* strike with the fist; pummel
 111 *pisspot metal* the pewter from which pisspots were commonly
     made

---

 108 *Sweet Oliver.* The stock epithet for 'mad' Orlando's rival in Ariosto's
     Orlando Furioso. Kno'well tries to move the 'merry' magistrate by
     indulging in his own type of idiotic repartee.

the bowers of sweet ladies, the cabins of soldiers! Roger,
away with him, by God's precious—I say, go to.   115

COB

Dear Master Justice; let me be beaten again, I have
deserved it: but not the prison, I beseech you.

KNO'WELL

Alas, poor Oliver!

CLEMENT

Roger, make him a warrant. He shall not go: I but fear the
knave.   120

FORMAL

Do not stink, sweet Oliver, you shall not go, my master
will give you a warrant.

COB

Oh, the Lord maintain his worship, his worthy worship.

CLEMENT

Away, dispatch him.   [*Exeunt* FORMAL *and* COB]
How now, Master Kno'well! In dumps? In dumps! Come,   125
this becomes not.

KNO'WELL

Sir, would I could not feel my cares—

CLEMENT

Your cares are nothing! They are like my cap, soon put on,
and as soon put off. What? Your son is old enough, to
govern himself: let him run his course, it's the only way to 130
make him a staid man. If he were an unthrift, a ruffian, a
drunkard, or a licentious liver, then you had reason; you had
reason to take care: but, being none of these, mirth's my
witness, an' I had twice so many cares, as you have, I'd
drown them all in a cup of sack. Come, come, let's try it: 135
I muse, your parcel of a soldier returns not all this while.

                                                    [*Exeunt*]

119 *fear* frighten
125 *In dumps?* 'Are you melancholy?'
131 *staid* a pun on 'stayed' ('run his course')

---

115 *by God's precious*. Clement has just contemptuously reprimanded Cob
    for swearing by God (l. 104): now he has to check himself in the use of a
    similar oath.
121 *sweet Oliver*. Parodying old Kno'well.
135 *sack*. A generic name for white wine imported from Spain and the
    Canaries; usually, however, it means sherry.
136 *parcel*. Part; an allusion to the unkempt appearance of Brainworm in his
    soldier's disguise—and a tribute to the efficacy of the disguise itself.

Act IV, Scene i

[*A Room in* KITELY'S *House*]

[*Enter*] DOWNRIGHT [*and*] DAME KITELY

DOWNRIGHT
Well sister, I tell you true: and you'll find it so, in the end.

DAME KITELY
Alas brother, what would you have me to do? I cannot help
it: you see, my brother brings 'hem in, here, they are his
friends.

DOWNRIGHT
His friends? His fiends. 'Slud, they do nothing but haunt   5
him, up and down, like a sort of unlucky sprites, and tempt
him to all manner of villainy, that can be thought of. Well,
by this light, a little thing would make me play the devil
with some of 'hem; and 'twere not more for your husband's
sake, than anything else, I'd make the house too hot for the   10
best on 'hem: they should say, and swear, hell were broken
loose, ere they went hence. But, by God's will, 'tis nobody's
fault, but yours: for, an' you had done, as you might have
done, they should have been parboiled, and baked too,
every mother's son, ere they should ha' come in, e'er a one   15
of 'hem.

DAME KITELY
God's my life! Did you ever hear the like? What a strange
man is this! Could I keep out all them, think you? I should
put myself, against half a dozen men? Should I? Good faith,
you'd mad the patient'st body in the world, to hear you talk   20
so, without any sense, or reason!

   [*Enter*] MISTRESS BRIDGET, MASTER MATTHEW, [*and*]
   BOBADILL; [*followed, at a little distance, by*] WELL-
   BRED, STEPHEN, ED. KNO'WELL [*and*] BRAINWORM

BRIDGET
Servant, in troth, you are too prodigal

---

   5 *'Slud* S'lud, F1: a further corruption of 'God's lid'
  14 *parboiled* thoroughly boiled (late Latin, *perbullire*); the modern
     sense, which goes back to the Fifteenth Century, comes from a
     confusion with 'part boiled'
  22 begins Act IV, Scene ii in Ff

---

  22 *Servant.* A common form of address to an authorized admirer; but
     there is some quiet irony in Bridget's attitude to Matthew: Jonson's
     question mark at the end of the speech makes this clear.

Of your wit's treasure, thus to pour it forth,
Upon so mean a subject, as my worth?

MATTHEW

You say well, mistress; and I mean, as well.   25

DOWNRIGHT

Hoy-day, here is stuff!

WELLBRED

Oh, now stand close: pray heaven, she can get him to read:
he should do it, of his own natural impudency.

BRIDGET

Servant, what is this same, I pray you?

MATTHEW

Marry, an elegy, an elegy, an odd toy—   30

DOWNRIGHT

To mock an ape withal. Oh, I could sew up his mouth, now.

DAME KITELY

Sister, I pray you let's hear it.

DOWNRIGHT

Are you rhyme-given, too?

MATTHEW

Mistress, I'll read it, if you please.

BRIDGET

Pray you do, servant.   35

DOWNRIGHT

Oh, here's no foppery! Death, I can endure the stocks,
better.   [*Exit*]

ED. KNO'WELL

What ails thy brother? Can he not hold his water, at reading
of a ballad?

WELLBRED

Oh, no: a rhyme to him, is worse than cheese, or a bagpipe.   40
But, mark, you lose the protestation.

MATTHEW

Faith, I did it in a humour; I know not how it is: but, please
you come near, sir. This gentleman has judgement, he knows
how to censure of a—pray you sir, you can judge.

STEPHEN

Not I, sir: upon my reputation, and, by the foot of Pharaoh.   45

36 *Oh . . . foppery* 'This is beyond folly'

---

25 *and . . . well.* Matthew is trying to get the subject round to his own
   verse: we are to imagine him pulling out his manuscript at this point.
26 *Hoy-day . . . stuff.* This expresses boredom and impatience, in contrast to Ed. Kno'well's and Wellbred's delight.
31 *To . . . withal.* Downright knows perfectly well what is going on, but he
   has all the irritation of an older man, not only at Matthew, but also at
   the mockers; by such touches Jonson adds psychological verisimilitude.

WELLBRED

Oh, chide your cousin, for swearing.

ED. KNO'WELL

Not I, so long as he does not foreswear himself.

BOBADILL

Master Matthew, you abuse the expectation of your dear
mistress, and her fair sister: fie, while you live, avoid this
prolixity.   50

MATTHEW

I shall, sir: well, *incipere dulce.*

ED. KNO'WELL

How! *Insipere dulce?* A sweet thing to be a fool, indeed.

WELLBRED

What, do you take *incipere,* in that sense?

ED. KNO'WELL

You do not? You? This was your villainy, to gull him with a
mot.   55

WELLBRED

Oh, the benchers' phrase: *pauca verba, pauca verba.*

MATTHEW

Rare creature, let me speak without offence,
Would God my rude words had the influence,
To rule thy thoughts, as thy fair looks do mine,
Then should'st thou be his prisoner, who is thine.   60

ED. KNO'WELL

This is in *Hero and Leander.*

WELLBRED

Oh, ay! Peace, we shall have more of this.

MATTHEW

Be not unkind, and fair, misshapen stuff
Is of behaviour boisterous, and rough.

WELLBRED

How like you that, sir?   65

MASTER STEPHEN *answers with shaking his head*

---

55 mot word; tag

---

51 incipere dulce. 'It is sweet to begin': the 'c' of 'incipere' was pronounced as an 's', making it identical with 'insipere' (l. 52): 'to be a fool'.
56 *Oh . . . verba.* 'Benchers' were loungers in alehouses, whose catch-
   phrase was *pauca verba,* i.e. 'less talk, more drink'.
57–60 *Rare creature . . . thine.* These four lines, and the next four Matthew
   reads out, are an inaccurate quotation from Marlowe's *Hero and Leander*
   (written *c.* 1592–1593, published 1598), which had become a lovers'
   handbook. Matthew offers them as his original work.

ED. KNO'WELL

'Slight, he shakes his head like a bottle, to feel and there be
any brain in it!

MATTHEW

But observe the catastrophe, now,
And I in duty will exceed all other,
As you in beauty do excel love's mother.   70

ED. KNO'WELL

Well, I'll have him free of the wit-brokers, for he utters
nothing, but stol'n remnants.

WELLBRED

Oh, forgive it him.

ED. KNO'WELL

A filching rogue? Hang him. And, from the dead? It's worse
than sacrilege.   75

[WELLBRED, ED. KNO'WELL *and* STEPHEN *come forward*]

WELLBRED

Sister, what ha' you here? Verses? Pray you, let's see. Who
made these verses? They are excellent good!

MATTHEW

Oh, Master Wellbred, 'tis your disposition to say so sir.
They were good i' the morning, I made 'hem, extempore,
this morning.   80

WELLBRED

How? Extempore?

MATTHEW

I would I might be hanged else; ask Captain Bobadill. He
saw me write them, at the—pox on it!—the Star, yonder.

BRAINWORM

Can he find, in his heart, to curse the stars, so?

ED. KNO'WELL

Faith, his are even with him: they ha' cursed him enough   85
already.

STEPHEN

Cousin, how do you like this gentleman's verses?

ED. KNO'WELL

Oh, admirable! The best that ever I heard, coz!

STEPHEN

Body o' Caesar! They are admirable! The best, that ever I
heard, as I am a soldier.   90

68 *catastrophe* 'climax' or 'conclusion' is meant
71 *free of* admitted to

74 *from the dead.* Marlowe was killed in 1593.

[*Enter* DOWNRIGHT]

DOWNRIGHT

I am vexed, I can hold ne'er a bone of me still! Heart! I
think, they mean to build, and breed here!

WELLBRED

Sister, you have a simple servant, here, that crowns your
beauty, with such encomiums, and devices: you may see,
what it is to be the mistress of a wit that can make your   95
perfections so transparent, that every blear eye may look
through them, and see him drowned over head, and ears, in
the deep well of desire. Sister Kitely, I marvel, you get you
not a servant, that can rhyme, and do tricks, too.

DOWNRIGHT

Oh monster! Impudence itself! Tricks?   100

DAME KITELY

Tricks, brother? What tricks?

BRIDGET

Nay, speak, I pray you, what tricks?

DAME KITELY

Ay, never spare any body here; but say, what tricks?

BRIDGET

Passion of my heart! Do tricks?

WELLBRED

'Slight, here's a trick vied, and revied! Why, you monkeys,   105
you? What a caterwauling do you keep? Has he not given
you rhymes, and verses, and tricks?

DOWNRIGHT

Oh, the fiend!

WELLBRED

Nay, you—lamp of virginity, that take it in snuff so! Come,
and cherish this tame 'poetical fury', in your servant, you'll 110
be begged else, shortly, for a concealment: go to, reward his
muse. You cannot give him less than a shilling, in conscience,

---

105 *vied, and revied* betted on, and then re-betted on (i.e. 'seen')
109 *take it in snuff* take offence at it (the smoking snuff of a candle was
    unpleasant)

---

99 *do tricks.* i.e. have sexual intercourse: the pun is on the Latin 'meretrix':
   whore.
109 *you—* you, Ff. Jonson's comma signified a pause while a fitting epithet
    was selected.
111 *begged . . . concealment.* In 1572 and 1579 Queen Elizabeth withdrew,
    on account of their abuse, her commissions for concealments—the
    retrieving of old monastery lands that had been retained in private
    hands, nominally for the crown, but in fact for the use of the courtiers
    who were appointed.

for the book, he had it out of, cost him a teston, at least.
How now, gallants? Master Matthew? Captain? What? All
sons of silence? No spirit?   115

DOWNRIGHT

Come, you might practise your ruffian-tricks somewhere
else, and not here, I wuss; this is no tavern, nor drinking-
school, to vent your exploits in.

WELLBRED

How now! Whose cow has calved?

DOWNRIGHT

Marry, that has mine, sir. Nay, boy, never look askance at   120
me, for the matter; I'll tell you of it, I, sir, you, and your
companions, mend yourselves, when I ha' done.

WELLBRED

My companions?

DOWNRIGHT

Yes sir, your companions, so I say, I am not afraid of you, nor
them neither: your hang-byes here. You must have your   125
poets, and your potlings, your soldados, and foolados, to
follow you up and down the city, and here they must come to
domineer, and swagger. Sirrah, you, ballad-singer, and
slops, your fellow there, get you out; get you home: or, by
this steel, I'll cut off your ears, and that, presently.   130

WELLBRED

'Slight, stay, let's see what he dare do: cut off his ears? Cut a
whetstone. You are an ass, do you see? Touch any man here,
and by this hand, I'll run my rapier to the hilts in you.

DOWNRIGHT

Yea, that would I fain see, boy.

They all draw, and they of the house make out to part them

DAME KITELY

Oh Jesu! Murder. Thomas, Gaspar!   135

BRIDGET

Help, help, Thomas.

---

113 *teston* tester: sixpence, the price of a play in Quarto
126 *potlings* inn-loungers
    soldados alluding contemptuously to Bobadill
    foolados a nonce-word of Downright's own invention
131–132 *cut a whetstone* i.e. 'a likely boast!'; a whetstone was the
    reward given to the person who told the biggest lie

---

117 *I wuss.* 'Gewiss' in Old English meant 'certainly'; the 'ge' became 'y'
    and was thus confused with 'I', so that 'I wiss' or 'wuss' was used to
    mean 'I know', or rather, as here, 'I'm certain'. See I.i, 34 n.
129 *slops.* i.e. Bobadill. with his huge breeches.

[Enter] CASH *[and* SERVANTS]

ED. KNO'WELL

Gentlemen, forebear, I pray you.

BOBADILL

Well, sirrah, you, Holofernes: by my hand, I will pink your
flesh, full of holes, with my rapier for this; I will, by this good
heaven (*They offer to fight again, and are parted*): nay, let him   140
come, let him come, gentlemen, by the body of St. George,
I'll not kill him.

CASH

Hold, hold, good gentlemen.

DOWNRIGHT

You whoreson, bragging coystril.

[Enter] KITELY

KITELY

Why, how now? What's the matter? What's the stir here?   145
Whence springs this quarrel? Thomas! Where is he?
Put up your weapons, and put off this rage.
My wife and sister, they are the cause of this,
What, Thomas? Where is this knave?

CASH   Here, sir.

WELLBRED

Come, let's go: this is one of my brother's ancient humours,   150
this.

STEPHEN

I am glad, nobody was hurt by his ancient humour.

[Exeunt WELLBRED, STEPHEN, ED. KNO'WELL, MATTHEW,
BOBADILL *and* BRAINWORM]

KITELY

Why, how now, brother, who enforced this brawl?

DOWNRIGHT

A sort of lewd rakehells, that care neither for God, nor the
devil! And, they must come here to read ballads, and   155
roguery, and trash! I'll mar the knot of 'hem ere I sleep,
perhaps: especially Bob, there: he that's all manner of
shapes! And 'Songs, and sonnets', his fellow.

138 *Holofernes* Bobadill means 'tyrant'
144 *coystril* rogue; originally 'custrel', an attendant on a knight:
      gained its meaning here from association with 'custron': scullion
145 begins Act IV, Scene iii in Ff
150 *ancient* old-fashioned; out-of-date

---

s.d. *Matthew*. Neither G nor any of the editors following him, except N by
      implication (because he follows Jonson's scene-divisions, and does not
      supply any s.d.'s at ends of scenes), dispose of Matthew, who would
      thus wrongly be left on stage until the end of the scene.
158 *shapes*. Another allusion to Bobadill's breeches.

BRIDGET
  Brother, indeed, you are too violent,
  Too sudden, in your humour: and, you know   160
  My brother Wellbred's temper will not bear
  Any reproof, chiefly in such a presence,
  Where every slight disgrace, he should receive,
  Might wound him in opinion, and respect.
DOWNRIGHT
  Respect? What talk you of respect 'mong such,   165
  As ha' nor spark of manhood, nor good manners?
  'Sdeins I am ashamed, to hear you! Respect?   [*Exit*]
BRIDGET
  Yes, there was one a civil gentleman,
  And very worthily demeaned himself!
KITELY
  Oh, that was some love of yours, sister!   170
BRIDGET
  A love of mine? I would it were no worse, brother!
  You'd pay my portion sooner, than you think for.
DAME KITELY
  Indeed, he seemed to be a gentleman of an exceeding fair
  disposition, and of very excellent good parts!
                    [*Exeunt* DAME KITELY *and* BRIDGET]
KITELY
  [*Aside*] Her love, by heaven! My wife's minion!   175
  Fair disposition? Excellent good parts?
  Death, these phrases are intolerable!
  Good parts? How should she know his parts?
  His parts? Well, well, well, well, well, well!
  It is too plain, too clear.—Thomas, come hither.   180
  What, are they gone?
CASH   Ay, sir, they went in.
  My mistress, and your sister—
KITELY
  Are any of the gallants within?
CASH
  No, sir, they are all gone.
KITELY
  Art thou sure of it?   185
CASH
  I can assure you, sir.

174 *parts* attributes; capacities
175 *minion* paramour

178–179 *Good parts . . . His parts?* Kitely morbidly dwells on the sexual
  sense of 'parts': 'private parts'.

KITELY

What gentleman was that they praised so, Thomas?

CASH

One, they call him Master Kno'well, a handsome young
gentleman, sir.

KITELY

[*Aside*] Ay, I thought so: my mind gave me as much.   190
I'll die, but they have hid him i' the house,
Somewhere; I'll go and search.—Go with me, Thomas.
Be true to me, and thou shalt find me a master.   [*Exeunt*]

Act IV, Scene [ii]

[*The Lane before* COB'S *House*]

[*Enter*] COB

COB

[*Knocking*] What Tib, Tib, I say!

TIB

[*From within*] How now, what cuckold is that knocks so
hard? [*She opens the door*] Oh, husband, is't you? What's the
news?

COB

Nay, you have stunned me, i' faith! You ha' gi'en me a   5
knock o' the forehead, will stick by me! Cuckold? 'Slid,
cuckold?

TIB

Away, you fool, did I know it was you, that knocked? Come,
come, you may call me as bad, when you list.

COB

May I? Tib, you are a whore.   10

TIB

You lie in your throat, husband.

COB

How, the lie? And in my throat too? Do you long to be
stabbed, ha?

TIB

Why, you are no soldier, I hope?

COB

Oh, must you be stabbed by a soldier? Mass, that's true!   15

---

191 *but they have* 'if they have not'
    Scene [*ii*] Scene iv in Ff

---

15 *Oh . . . soldier*. There are sexual overtones in the use of the term
'stab' here; Cob's suspicious jealousy is a comic parody of Kitely's.

When was Bobadill here? Your captain? That rogue, that
foist, that fencing Burgullian? I'll tickle him, i' faith.

TIB

Why, what's the matter? Trow!

COB

Oh, he has basted me, rarely, sumptuously! But I have it
here in black and white; [*Pulls out his warrant*] for his black,   20
and blue: shall pay him. Oh, the Justice! The honestest old
brave Trojan in London! I do honour the very flea of his
dog. A plague on him though, he put me once in a villainous
filthy fear; marry, it vanished away, like the smoke of
tobacco; but I was smoked soundly first. I thank the devil,   25
and his good angel, my guest. Well, wife, or Tib—which
you will—get you in, and lock the door, I charge you, let
nobody in to you; wife, no body in, to you: those are my
words. Not Captain Bob himself, nor the fiend, in his likeness; you are a woman; you have flesh and blood enough in   30
you, to be tempted: therefore, keep the door, shut, upon all
comers.

TIB

I warrant you, there shall nobody enter here, without my
consent.

COB

Nor with your consent, sweet Tib, and so I leave you.   35

TIB

It's more, than you know, whether you leave me so.

COB

How?

TIB

Why, sweet.

COB

Tut, sweet, or sour, thou art a flower, [*Kissing her*]
Keep close thy door, I ask no more.   [*Exeunt*]   40

---

17 *foist* cut-purse: cheat
20 *black and white* referring to his warrant
21 *pay* punish; pay him back: 'he will be paid back for the thrashing
    he gave me'
25 *I . . . first* 'I had a hot time of it first'

---

17 *fencing Burgullian.* Bully: a Burgonian, or Burgundian, John Barrose,
    who challenged all the fencers of England, was hanged for murdering a
    city-officer on 10 July, 1598.
28 *no body.* Here Bobadill quibbles obscenely on the first 'nobody'; F1 of
    course reads 'no body' throughout.

Act IV, Scene [iii]

[A Room in the Windmill Tavern]

[*Enter*] ED. KNO'WELL, WELLBRED, STEPHEN [*and*] BRAINWORM
[*disguised as before*]

ED. KNO'WELL

Well Brainworm, perform this business, happily, and thou
makest a purchase of my love, forever.

WELLBRED

I' faith, now let thy spirits use their best faculties. But, at
any hand, remember the message, to my brother: for, there's
no other means, to start him.   5

BRAINWORM

I warrant you, sir, fear nothing: I have a nimble soul has
waked all forces of my phant'sie, by this time, and put 'hem
in true motion. What you have possessed me withal, I'll
discharge it amply, sir. Make it no question.

WELLBRED

Forth, and prosper, Brainworm. [*Exit* BRAINWORM] Faith,   10
Ned, how dost thou approve of my abilities in this device?

ED. KNO'WELL

Troth, well, howsoever: but, it will come excellent, if it take.

WELLBRED

Take, man? Why, it cannot choose but take, if the circumstances miscarry not: but, tell me, ingenuously, dost thou
affect my sister Bridget, as thou pretend'st?   15

ED. KNO'WELL

Friend, am I worth belief?

WELLBRED

Come, do not protest. In faith, she is a maid of good orna-
ment, and much modesty: and, except I conceived very
worthily of her, thou shouldest not have her.

ED. KNO'WELL

Nay, that I am afraid will be a question yet, whether I shall   20
have her, or no?

WELLBRED

'Slid, thou shalt have her; by this light, thou shalt.

ED. KNO'WELL

Nay, do not swear.

Scene [iii] Scene v in Ff
12 *howsoever* whatever happens
15 *pretend'st* used here in one of its original, non-pejorative, senses:
   'to put forth an assertion about oneself'—we should say, 'as you
   say'

WELLBRED

By this hand, thou shalt have her: I'll go fetch her, presently. Point, but where to meet, and as I am an honest man,   25
I'll bring her.

ED. KNO'WELL

Hold, hold, be temperate.

WELLBRED

Why, by—what shall I swear by? Thou shalt have her, as
I am—

ED. KNO'WELL

'Pray thee, be at peace, I am satisfied: and do believe, thou   30
wilt omit no offered occasion, to make my desires complete.

WELLBRED

Thou shalt see, and know, I will not.

Act IV, Scene iv

[The Old Jewry]

[Enter] FORMAL *[and]* KNO'WELL

FORMAL

Was your man a soldier, sir?

KNO'WELL

Ay, a knave, I took him begging o' the way,
This morning, as I came over Moorfields!
Oh, here he is! Yo' have made fair speed, believe me:
Where, i' the name of sloth, could you be thus—   5

[Enter BRAINWORM, disguised as before]

BRAINWORM

Marry, peace be my comfort, where I thought I should have
had so little comfort of your worship's service.

KNO'WELL

How so?

BRAINWORM

Oh, sir! Your coming to the city, your entertainment of me,
and your sending me to watch—indeed, all the circum-   10
stances either of your charge, or my employment, are as open
to your son, as to yourself!

KNO'WELL

How should that be! Unless that villain, Brainworm,
Have told him of the letter, and discovered
All that I strictly charged him to conceal? 'Tis so!   15

BRAINWORM

I am, partly, o' the faith, 'tis so indeed.

KNO'WELL

But, how should he know thee to be my man?

BRAINWORM

Nay, sir, I cannot tell; unless it be by the black art! Is not
your son a scholar, sir?

KNO'WELL

Yes, but I hope his soul is not allied   20
Unto such hellish practices: if it were,
I had just cause to weep my part in him,
And curse the time of his creation.
But, where didst thou find them, Fitzsword?

BRAINWORM

You should rather ask, where they found me, sir, for, I'll be   25
sworn I was going along in the street, thinking nothing,
when, of a sudden, a voice calls, 'Master Kno'well's man!';
another cries, 'Soldier!': and thus, half a dozen of 'hem, till
they had called me within a house where I no sooner came,
but they seemed men, and out flew all their rapiers at my   30
bosom, with some three or fourscore oaths to accompany
'hem, and all to tell me, I was but a dead man, if I did not
confess where you were, and how I was employed, and
about what; which, when they could not get out of me—as I
protest, they must ha' dissected, and made an anatomy o'me,   35
first, and so I told 'hem—they locked me up into a room i'
the top of a high house, whence, by great miracle, having a
light heart, I slid down, by a bottom of packthread, into the
street, and so scaped. But, sir, thus much I can assure you,
for I heard it, while I was locked up, there were a great   40
many rich merchants, and brave citizens' wives with 'hem at
a feast, and your son, Master Edward, withdrew with one of
'hem, and has pointed to meet her anon, at one Cob's house,
a water-bearer, that dwells by the wall. Now, there, your
worship shall be sure to take him, for there he preys, and   45
fail he will not.

KNO'WELL

Nor, will I fail, to break his match, I doubt not.
Go thou, along with Justice Clement's man,
And stay there for me. At one Cob's house, say'st thou?

30 *they seemed men* they appeared as men—i.e. they had been voices
    before, now they materialized as men
35 *anatomy* a subject for dissection
38 *bottom of packthread* ball of twine
41 *brave* richly dressed

19 *scholar*. In the mind of such a person as Brainworm is impersonating,
    'scholarship' was of course associated with necromancy; old Kno'well
    takes Brainworm's suggestion seriously.

BRAINWORM
Ay sir, there you shall have him.   [*Exit* KNO'WELL]   50
[*Aside*] Yes? Invisible? Much wench, or much son? 'Slight,
when he has stayed there, three or four hours, travailing
with the expectation of wonders, and at length be delivered
of air: Oh, the sport, that I should then take, to look on him,
if I durst! But, now, I mean to appear no more afore him in   55
this shape. I have another trick, to act, yet. Oh, that I were
so happy; as to light on a nupson, now, of this Justice's
novice.—Sir, I make you stay somewhat long.

FORMAL
Not a whit, sir. 'Pray you, what do you mean? Sir?

BRAINWORM
I was putting up some papers—   60

FORMAL
You ha' been lately in the wars, sir, it seems.

BRAINWORM
Marry have I, sir; to my loss: and expense of all, almost—

FORMAL
Troth sir, I would be glad to bestow a pottle of wine o'you,
if it please you to accept it—

BRAINWORM
Oh, sir—   65

FORMAL
But, to hear the manner of your services, and your devices in
the wars, they say they be very strange, and not like those a
man reads in the Roman histories, or sees, at Mile End.

BRAINWORM
No, I assure you, sir, why, at any time when it please you, I
shall be ready to discourse to you, all I know: [*Aside*] and   70
more too, somewhat.

FORMAL
No better time, than now, sir; we'll go to the Windmill:
there we shall have a cup of neat grist, we call it. I pray you,
sir, let me request you, to the Windmill.

---

51 *much* equivalent to the modern ironic 'a lot of . . .'
57 *nupson* fool; gull
63 *pottle* two quarts

---

68 *Roman histories.* Either North's *Plutarch* (1579) or, more likely, more
   popular compilations, containing gobbets of Roman history.
   Mile End. The city's militia manoeuvres, like most military exercises in
   peacetime, were much laughed at; only the very unsophisticated, as
   Formal, could be relied upon to take them seriously.
73 *grist.* Malt; but here used for the beer itself. Brainworm puns on this in
   his reply.

BRAINWORM

I'll follow you, sir, [*Aside*] and make grist o' you, if I have   75
good luck.

Act IV, Scene [v]

[*Moorfields*]

[*Enter*] MATTHEW, ED. KNO'WELL, BOBADILL [*and*] STEPHEN

MATTHEW

Sir, did your eyes ever taste the like clown of him, where we
were today, Master Wellbred's half-brother? I think, the
whole earth cannot show his parallel, by this daylight.

ED. KNO'WELL

We were now speaking of him: Captain Bobadill tells me,
he is fall'n foul o' you, too.   5

MATTHEW

Oh, ay, sir, he threatened me, with the bastinado.

BOBADILL

Ay, but I think, I taught you prevention, this morning, for
that— You shall kill him, beyond question: if you be so
generously minded.

MATTHEW

Indeed, it is a most excellent trick! [*Fences*]   10

BOBADILL

Oh, you do not give spirit enough, to your motion, you are
too tardy, too heavy! Oh, it must be done like lightning, hay?
(*He practises at a post*)

MATTHEW

Rare Captain!

BOBADILL

Tut, 'tis nothing, and't be not done in a—*punto*!

ED. KNO'WELL

Captain, did you ever prove yourself, upon any of our   15
masters of defence, here?

MATTHEW

Oh, good sir! Yes, I hope, he has.

BOBADILL

I will tell you, sir. Upon my first coming to the city, after my
long travail, for knowledge—in that mystery only—there
came three, or four of 'hem to me, at a gentleman's house,   20

Scene [v] Scene vii in Ff
12 *hay?* the Italian 'hai', 'thou hast it!' on hitting an opponent in
    fencing
14 *punto*! instant; also, 'a thrust with the point'
19 *travail* quibbling on the two senses of 'labour' and 'travel'

where it was my chance to be resident, at that time, to
entreat my presence at their schools, and withal so much
importuned me, that—I protest to you as I am a gentleman
—I was ashamed of their rude demeanour, out of all
measure: well, I told 'hem, that to come to a public school,   25
they should pardon me, it was opposite, in diameter, to my
humour, but, if so they would give their attendance at my
lodging, I protested to do them what right or favour I could,
as I was a gentleman, and so forth.

ED. KNO'WELL

So, sir, then you tried their skill?   30

BOBADILL

Alas, soon tried! You shall hear sir. Within two or three
days after, they came; and, by honesty, fair sir, believe me,
I graced them exceedingly, showed them some two or three
tricks of prevention, have purchased 'hem, since, a credit, to
admiration! They cannot deny this: and yet now, they hate   35
me, and why? Because I am excellent, and for no other vile
reason on the earth.

ED. KNO'WELL

This is strange, and barbarous! As ever I heard!

BOBADILL

Nay, for a more instance of their preposterous natures, but
note, sir. They have assaulted me some three, four, five, six   40
of them together, as I have walked alone, in divers skirts i'
the town, as Turnbull, Whitechapel, Shoreditch, which were
then my quarters, and since upon the Exchange, at my
lodging, and at my ordinary: where I have driven them afore
me, the whole length of a street, in the open view of all our   45
gallants, pitying to hurt them, believe me. Yet all this lenity
will not o'ercome their spleen: they will be doing with the
pismire, raising a hill, a man may spurn abroad, with his
foot, at pleasure. By myself, I could have slain them all, but
I delight not in murder. I am loath to bear any other than   50
this bastinado for 'hem: yet, I hold it good polity, not to go
disarmed, for though I be skilful, I may be oppressed with
multitudes.

26 *in diameter* in direct opposition
47–48 *the pismire* (the pismier, F1) ant; H & S reads 'a pismier';
    presumably this is a misprint
51 *bastinado* here refers to the cudgel itself

42 *Turnbull.* Turnmill Street, near Clerkenwell Green, a noted haunt of
    prostitutes. Both Whitechapel and Shoreditch had somewhat similar
    reputations: Bobadill has forgotten his man-of-fashion's sensitivity.

ED. KNO'WELL

> Ay, believe me, may you sir: and, in my conceit, our whole
> nation should sustain the loss by it, if it were so.   55

BOBADILL

> Alas, no: what's a peculiar man, to a nation? Not seen.

ED. KNO'WELL

> Oh, but your skill, sir!

BOBADILL

> Indeed, that might be some loss; but, who respects it? I will
> tell you, sir, by the way of private, and under seal; I am a
> gentleman, and live here obscure, and to myself; but, were   60
> I known to Her Majesty, and the Lords—observe me—I
> would undertake, upon this poor head, and life, for the
> public benefit of the state, not only to spare the entire lives
> of her subjects in general, but to save the one half, nay, three
> parts of her yearly charge, in holding war, and against what   65
> enemy soever. And, how would I do it, think you?

ED. KNO'WELL

> Nay, I know not, nor can I conceive.

BOBADILL

> Why thus, sir. I would select nineteen, more, to myself,
> throughout the land; gentlemen they should be of good
> spirit, strong, and able constitution, I would choose them by   70
> an instinct, a character, that I have: and I would teach these
> nineteen, the special rules, as your punto, your reverso, your
> stoccata, your imbroccata, your passada, your montanto: till
> they could all play very near, or altogether as well as myself.
> This done, say the enemy were forty thousand strong, we   75
> twenty would come into the field, the tenth of March, or
> thereabouts; and we would challenge twenty of the enemy;
> they could not, in their honour, refuse us, well, we would
> kill them: challenge twenty more, kill them; twenty more,
> kill them; twenty more, kill them too; and thus, would we   80
> kill, every man, his twenty a day, that's twenty score;
> twenty score, that's two hundred; two hundred a day, five
> days a thousand; forty thousand; forty times five, five times
> forty, two hundred days kills them all up, by computation.
> And this, will I venture my poor gentleman-like carcass, to   85

54 *conceit* opinion
56 *peculiar* special; singular
72 *reverso* a back stroke
73 *imbroccata* a high, downwards thrust sent in over the opponent's
   sword or dagger
   montanto an upwards thrust
82 *that's two hundred* this error worried G, who finally decided
   that Jonson must have intended it

perform—provided there be no treason practised upon us—
by fair, and discreet manhood, that is, civilly by the sword.

ED. KNO'WELL

Why, are you so sure of your hand, Captain, at all times?

BOBADILL

Tut, never miss thrust, upon my reputation with you.

ED. KNO'WELL

I would not stand in Downright's state, then, an' you meet   90
him, for the wealth of any one street in London.

BOBADILL

Why, sir, you mistake me! If he were here now, by this
welkin, I would not draw my weapon on him! Let this gentleman do his mind: but, I will bastinado him, by the bright
sun, wherever I meet him.   95

MATTHEW

Faith, and I'll have a fling at him, at my distance.

ED. KNO'WELL

God's so', look, where he is: yonder he goes.

> DOWNRIGHT *walks over the stage*

DOWNRIGHT

What peevish luck have I, I cannot meet with those
bragging rascals?   [*Exit*]

BOBADILL

It's not he? Is it?   100

ED. KNO'WELL

Yes faith, it is he.

MATTHEW

I'll be hanged, then, if that were he.

ED. KNO'WELL

Sir, keep your hanging good, for some greater matter, for I
assure you, that was he.

STEPHEN

Upon my reputation, it was he.   105

BOBADILL

Had I thought it had been he, he must not have gone so: but
I can hardly be induced, to believe, it was he, yet.

ED. KNO'WELL

That I think, sir.

> [*Enter* DOWNRIGHT]

But see, he is come again!

DOWNRIGHT

Oh, Pharaoh's foot, have I found you? Come, draw, to your   110
tools: draw, gipsy, or I'll thrash you.

---

87 *civilly* in a gentlemanly fashion
111 *tools* rapier and dagger   *gipsy* lying rogue

BOBADILL
Gentleman of valour, I do believe in thee, hear me—
DOWNRIGHT
Draw your weapon, then.
BOBADILL
Tall man, I never thought on it, till now—body of me—I
had a warrant of the peace, served on me, even now, as I   115
came along, by a water-bearer; this gentleman saw it,
Master Matthew.
DOWNRIGHT
'Sdeath, you will not draw, then?

He beats him, and disarms him: MATTHEW *runs away*

BOBADILL
Hold, hold, under thy favour, forbear.
DOWNRIGHT
Prate again, as you like this, you whoreson foist, you. You'll   120
control the point, you? Your consort is gone? Had he stayed,
he had shared with you, sir.   [*Exit*]
BOBADILL
Well, gentlemen, bear witness, I was bound to the peace, by
this good day.
ED. KNO'WELL
No faith, it's an ill day, Captain, never reckon it other: but,   125
say you were bound to the peace, the law allows you, to
defend yourself: that'll prove but a poor excuse.
BOBADILL
I cannot tell, sir. I desire good construction, in fair sort. I
never sustained the like disgrace, by heaven, sure I was struck
with a planet thence, for I had no power to touch my weapon.   130
ED. KNO'WELL
Ay, like enough, I have heard of many that have been beaten
under a planet: go, get you to a surgeon. [*Exit* BOBADILL]
'Slid, an' these be your tricks, your passadas, and your
montantos, I'll none of them. Oh, manners! That this age
should bring forth such creatures! That nature should be at   135
leisure to make' hem! Come, coz.
STEPHEN
Mass, I'll ha' this cloak.
ED. KNO'WELL
God's will, 'tis Downright's.

120 *foist* cheat
129–130 *struck with a planet* a convenient astrological excuse for any-
    thing that could not be explained
    thence suddenly

STEPHEN

Nay, it's mine now, another might have ta'en it up, as well as
I: I'll wear it, so I will.　　140

ED. KNO'WELL

How, an' he see it? He'll challenge it, assure yourself.

STEPHEN

Ay, but he shall not ha' it; I'll say, I bought it.

ED. KNO'WELL

Take heed, you buy it not, too dear, coz.　　[*Exeunt*]

Act IV, [Scene vi]

[A Room in KITELY'S *House]*

[Enter] KITELY, WELLBRED, DAME KITELY, [*and*] BRIDGET

KITELY

Now, trust me brother, you were much to blame,
T' incense his anger, and disturb the peace,
Of my poor house, where there are sentinels
That every minute watch, to give alarms,
Of civil war, without adjection　　5
Of your assistance, or occasion.

WELLBRED

No harm done, brother, I warrant you: since there is no
harm done. Anger costs a man nothing: and a tall man is
never his own man, till he be angry. To keep his valour in
obscurity, is to keep himself, as it were, in a cloak-bag.　　10
What's a musician, unless he play? What's a tall man,
unless he fight? For, indeed, all this, my wise brother stands
upon, absolutely: and, that made me fall in with him, so
resolutely.

DAME KITELY

Ay, but what harm might have come of it, brother?　　15

WELLBRED

Might, sister? So, might the good warm clothes, your
husband wears, be poisoned, for anything he knows: or the
wholesome wine he drunk, even now, at the table—

139 *ta'en it up*, F2, ta'en up, F1
　　Scene [vi] Scene vii in Ff
　　3–4 *where . . . alarms* 'where there are enough troubles already'
　　5 *adjection* addition

　　8–9 *and a tall man . . . angry.* 'A man of parts is never himself until he
　　gets a chance to prove himself': a courteous reference to the fact that
　　Downright has enjoyed losing his temper.

KITELY

    [*Aside*] Now, God forbid: Oh me. Now, I remember,
    My wife drunk to me, last: and changed the cup: 20
    And bade me wear this cursed suit today.
    See, if heavn' suffer murder undiscovered!—
    I feel me ill; give me some mithridate,
    Some mithridate and oil, good sister, fetch me;
    Oh, I am sick at heart! I burn, I burn.   25
    If you will save my life, go, fetch it me.

WELLBRED

    Oh, strange humour! My very breath has poisoned him.

BRIDGET

    Good brother, be content, what do you mean? The strength
    of these extreme conceits, will kill you.

DAME KITELY

    Beshrew your heart-blood, brother Wellbred, now;   30
    For putting such a toy into his head.

WELLBRED

    Is a fit simile, a toy? Will he be poisoned with a simile?
    Brother Kitely, what a strange, and idle imagination is this?
    For shame, be wiser. Oh my soul, there's no such matter.

KITELY

    Am I not sick? How am I, then, not poisoned? Am I not   35
    poisoned? How am I, then, so sick?

DAME KITELY

    If you be sick, your own thoughts make you sick.

WELLBRED

    His jealousy is the poison, he has taken.

        [*Enter*] BRAINWORM. *He comes disguised like Justice*
            Clement's man, [FORMAL]

BRAINWORM

    Master Kitely, my master, Justice Clement, salutes you;
    and desires to speak with you, with all possible speed.   40

KITELY

    No time, but now? When, I think, I am sick? Very sick!
    Well, I will wait upon his worship. Thomas, Cob! [*Aside*]
    I must seek them out, and set 'hem sentinels, till I return.—
    Thomas, Cob, Thomas.   [*Exit*]

WELLBRED

    [*Takes* BRAINWORM *aside*] This is perfectly rare, Brainworm! 45
    But how got'st thou this apparel, of the Justice's man?

---

23 *mithridate* a quack electuary, compounded of many ingredients,
    supposed to be an antidote to poison and infection

SCENE VI]   EVERY MAN IN HIS HUMOUR   103

BRAINWORM

Marry sir, my proper fine pen-man, would needs bestow
the grist o' me, at the Windmill, to hear some martial discourse; where so I marshalled him, that I made him drunk,
with admiration! And, because, too much heat was the cause   50
of his distemper, I stripped him stark naked, as he lay along
asleep, and borrowed his suit, to deliver this counterfeit
message in, leaving a rusty armour, and an old brown bill to
watch him, till my return: which shall be, when I ha'
pawned his apparel, and spent the better part o' the money,   55
perhaps.

WELLBRED

Well, thou art a successful merry knave, Brainworm, his
absence will be a good subject for more mirth. I pray thee,
return to thy young master, and will him to meet me, and
my sister Bridget, at the Tower instantly: for, here, tell him,   60
the house is so stored with jealousy, there is no room for
love, to stand upright in. We must get our fortunes committed to some larger prison, say; and, than the Tower, I
know no better air: nor where the liberty of the house may
do us more present service. Away.   [*Exit* BRAINWORM]   65

[*Enter* KITELY], CASH [*following*]

KITELY

Come hither, Thomas. Now, my secret's ripe,
And thou shalt have it: lay to both thine ears.
Hark, what I say to thee. I must go forth, Thomas.
Be careful of thy promise, keep good watch,
Note every gallant, and observe him well,   70
That enters in my absence, to thy mistress:
If she would show him rooms, the jest is stale,
Follow 'hem, Thomas, or else hang on him,
And let him not go after; mark their looks;
Note, if she offer but to see his band,   75
Or any other amorous toy, about him;
But praise his leg; or foot; or if she say,
The day is hot, and bid him feel her hand,
How hot it is; Oh, that's a monstrous thing!
Note me all this, good Thomas, mark their sighs,   80

47 *pen-man* clerk
53 *brown bill* a pike used by watchmen
72 *the jest is stale* 'that's an old story!'

60 *the Tower.* Until 1632 the Tower, being extra-parochial, could be used
for immediate private marriages.

And, if they do but whisper, break 'hem off:
I'll bear thee out in it. Wilt thou do this?
Will thou be true, my Thomas?

CASH   As truth's self, sir.

KITELY

Why, I believe thee: where is Cob, now? Cob?   [*Exit*]

DAME KITELY

He's ever calling for Cob! I wonder, how he employs Cob, so!   85

WELLBRED

Indeed, sister, to ask how he employs Cob, is a necessary
question for you, that are his wife, and a thing not very easy
for you to be satisfied in: but this I'll assure you, Cob's wife
is an excellent bawd, sister, and, oftentimes, your husband
haunts her house, marry, to what end, I cannot altogether   90
accuse him, imagine you what you think convenient. But,
I have known, fair hides have foul hearts, ere now, sister.

DAME KITELY

Never said you truer than that, brother, so much I can tell
you for your learning. Thomas, fetch your cloak, and go
with me, I'll after him presently. [*Exit* CASH] I would to   95
fortune, I could take him there, i' faith. I'd return him
his own, I warrant him.   [*Exit*]

WELLBRED

So, let 'hem go: this may make sport anon. Now, my fair
sister-in-law, that you knew, but how happy a thing it were
to be fair, and beautiful?   100

BRIDGET

That touches not me, brother.

WELLBRED

That's true; that's even the fault of it: for, indeed, beauty
stands a woman in no stead, unless it procure her touching.
But, sister, whether it touch you, or no, it touches your
beauties; and, I am sure, they will abide the touch; an' they   105
do not, a plague of all ceruse, say I: and, it touches me too in
part, though not in the— Well, there's a dear and respected
friend of mine, sister, stands very strongly, and worthily
affected toward you, and hath vowed to inflame whole bon-
fires of zeal, at his heart, in honour of your perfections. I   110
have already engaged my promise to bring you, where you
shall hear him confirm much more. Ned Kno'well is the man,

---

103 *touching* a quibble on the sexual sense

106 *ceruse*. White lead used for cosmetic purposes: Wellbred means 'a
curse on your cosmetics if they make you appear beautiful when you
are not!'.

107 *in the*—. Wellbred pretends to affect modesty.

sister. There's no exception against the party. You are ripe
for a husband; and a minute's loss to such an occasion, is a
great trespass in a wise beauty. What say you, sister? On   115
my soul he loves you. Will you give him the meeting?

BRIDGET

Faith, I had very little confidence in mine own constancy,
brother, if I durst not meet a man: but this motion of yours,
savours of an old knight-adventurer's servant, a little too
much, methinks.   120

WELLBRED

What's that, sister?

BRIDGET

Marry, of the squire.

WELLBRED

No matter if it did, I would be such an one for my friend,
but see! Who is returned to hinder us?

[*Enter* KITELY]

KITELY

What villainy is this? Called out on a false message?   125
There was some plot! I was not sent for. Bridget,
Where's your sister?

BRIDGET   I think she be gone forth, sir.

KITELY

How! Is my wife gone forth? Whither for God's sake?

BRIDGET

She's gone abroad with Thomas.

KITELY

Abroad with Thomas? Oh, that villain dors me.   130
He hath discovered all unto my wife!
Beast that I was, to trust him: whither, I pray you,
Went she?

BRIDGET

I know not, sir.

WELLBRED   I'll tell you, brother,
Whither I suspect she's gone.

KITELY   Whither, good brother?

WELLBRED

To Cob's house, I believe: but, keep my counsel.   135

KITELY

I will, I will: to Cob's house? Doth she haunt Cob's?
She's gone a' purpose, now, to cuckold me,

113 *There's . . . party* 'there's nothing against him'
122 *squire* pimp
130 *dors* deceives (dor: chafer beetle, which is wayward in its flight)

With that lewd rascal, who, to win her favour,
Hath told her all.   [*Exit*]
WELLBRED   Come, he's once more gone.
Sister, let's lose no time; th' affair is worth it.   [*Exeunt*]   140

Act IV, Scene [vii]

[*A Street*]

[*Enter*] MATTHEW [*and*] BOBADILL

MATTHEW
I wonder, Captain, what they will say of my going away?
Ha?
BOBADILL
Why, what should they say? But as of a discreet gentleman?
Quick, wary, respectful of nature's fair lineaments: and
that's all.   5
MATTHEW
Why, so! But what can they say of your beating?
BOBADILL
A rude part, a touch with soft wood, a kind of gross battery
used, laid on strongly, borne most patiently: and that's all.
MATTHEW
Ay, but, would any man have offered it in Venice? As you
say?   10
BOBADILL
Tut, I assure you, no: you shall have there your Nobilis, your
Gentilezza, come in bravely upon your reverse, stand you
close, stand you firm, stand you fair, save your retricato
with his left leg, come to the asalto with the right, thrust
with brave steel, defy your base wood! But, wherefore do I   15
awake this remembrance? I was fascinated, by Jupiter:
fascinated: but I will be unwitched, and revenged, by law.

Scene [*vii*] Scene ix in Ff
11–12 *Nobilis . . . Gentilezza* Latin adjective and Italian noun for
'gentlemen by title'
13 *retricato* there seems to have been no such word: it may be a
confusion with 'rintricato', entangled
17 *fascinated* bewitched
unwitched disenchanted; freed from the spell

9–10 *in Venice? As you say?* This is out of keeping with the scene of the F
revision, but Jonson needed to keep it in order to introduce Bobadill's
fantasy-world of *gentilezza*, etc. Jonson added the 'As you say?' in
order to presuppose some kind of a conversation between Matthew and
Bobadill on the subject.

MATTHEW

Do you hear? Is't not best to get a warrant, and have him
arrested, and brought before Justice Clement.

BOBADILL

It were not amiss, would we had it.   20

[Enter] BRAINWORM, [*disguised as* FORMAL]

MATTHEW

Why, here comes his man, let's speak to him.

BOBADILL

Agreed, do you speak.

MATTHEW

Save you, sir.

BRAINWORM

With all my heart, sir.

MATTHEW

Sir, there is one Downright, hath abused this gentleman, and   25
myself, and we determine to make our amends by law;
now, if you would do us the favour, to procure a warrant, to
bring afore your master, you shall be well considered, I
assure you, sir.

BRAINWORM

Sir, you know my service is my living, such favours as these,   30
gotten of my master, is his only preferment, and therefore,
you must consider me, as I may make benefit of my place.

MATTHEW

How is that, sir?

BRAINWORM

Faith sir, the thing is extraordinary, and the gentleman may
be, of great account: yet, be what he will, if you will lay me   35
down a brace of angels, in my hand, you shall have it, other-
wise not.

MATTHEW

How shall we do, Captain? He asks a brace of angels, you
have no money?

BOBADILL

Not a cross, by fortune.   40

MATTHEW

Nor I, as I am a gentleman, but twopence, left of my two
shillings in the morning for wine, and radish: let's find him
some pawn.

BOBADILL

Pawn? We have none to the value of his demand.

36 *a brace of angels* about a pound; far in excess of the lawful fee
40 *cross* the silver penny and halfpenny were marked with a cross;
   hence the quibble on 'fortune'

MATTHEW

Oh, yes. I'll pawn this jewel in my ear, and you may pawn   45
your silk stockings, and pull up your boots, they will ne'er
be missed: it must be done, now.

BOBADILL

Well, an' there be no remedy: I'll step aside, and pull 'hem
off.

MATTHEW

Do you hear, sir? We have no store of money at this time,   50
but you shall have good pawns: look you, sir, this jewel,
and that gentleman's silk stockings, because we would have
it dispatched, ere we went to our chambers.

BRAINWORM: I am content, sir; I will get you the warrant
presently, what's his name, say you? Downright?   55

MATTHEW

Ay, ay, George Downright.

BRAINWORM

What manner of man is he?

MATTHEW

A tall big man, sir; he goes in a cloak, most commonly, of
silk russet, laid about with russet lace.

BRAINWORM

'Tis very good, sir.   60

MATTHEW

Here sir, here's my jewel.

BOBADILL

And, here, are stockings.

BRAINWORM

Well, gentlemen, I'll procure you this warrant presently, but,
who will you have to serve it?

MATTHEW

That's true, Captain: that must be considered.   65

BOBADILL

Body o' me, I know not! 'Tis service of danger!

BRAINWORM

Why, you were best get one o' the varlets o' the city, a
sergeant. I'll appoint you one, if you please.

MATTHEW

Will you, sir? Why, we can wish no better.

BOBADILL

We'll leave it to you, sir. [*Exeunt* BOBADILL *and* MATTHEW]   70

59 *russet* a coarse cloth, usually worn by country folk, but also by
some townspeople of means
russet lace lace of a reddish brown colour
67 *varlets* originally servants of a knight; here bailiffs of the city
prisons, who carried a mace and wore a gown

BRAINWORM

This is rare! Now, will I go pawn this cloak of the Justice's
man's, at the brokers, for a varlet's suit, and be the varlet
myself; and get either more pawns, or more money of
Downright, for the arrest.   [*Exit*]

Act IV Scene [viii]

[*The Lane before* COB'S *House*]

[*Enter*] KNO'WELL

KNO'WELL

Oh, here it is, I am glad: I have found it now. Ho! Who is
within, here?   [*Knock* COB'S *door*]

TIB

[*From within*] I am within sir, what's your pleasure?

KNO'WELL

To know, who is within, besides yourself.

TIB

Why, sir, you are no constable, I hope?   5

KNO'WELL

Oh! Fear you the constable? Then, I doubt not,
You have some guests within, deserve that fear,
I'll fetch him straight.   [*Tib opens*]

TIB   O' God's name, sir.

KNO'WELL

Go to. Come, tell me, is not young Kno'well, here?

TIB

Young Kno'well? I know none such, sir, o' mine honesty!   10

KNO'WELL

Your honesty? Dame, it flies too lightly from you:
There is no way, but, fetch the constable.

TIB

The constable? The man is mad, I think.

[*Exit. Slams the door*]

[*Enter*] DAME KITELY [*and*] CASH

CASH

Ho, who keeps house, here?

KNO'WELL

Oh, this is the female copesmate of my son?   15
Now shall I meet him straight.

72 *for* instead of
   Scene [*viii*] Scene x in Ff
11 *it . . . you* 'you speak too lightly of honesty, which in any case
   you part with too easily (because you are a whore)'
15 *female copesmate* mistress; illicit lover

DAME KITELY   Knock, Thomas, hard.
CASH
  Ho, good wife?   [TIB *opens door a crack*]
TIB   Why, what's the matter with you?
DAME KITELY
  Why, woman, grieves it you to ope' your door?
  Belike, you get something, to keep it shut.
TIB
  What mean these questions, 'pray ye?   20
DAME KITELY
  So strange you make it? Is not my husband, here?
KNO'WELL
  Her husband!
DAME KITELY   My tried husband, Master Kitely.
TIB
  I hope, he needs not to be tried, here.
DAME KITELY
  No, dame: he does it not for need, but pleasure.
TIB
  Neither for need, nor pleasure, is he here.   25
KNO'WELL
  This is but a device, to baulk me withal.

      [Enter] KITELY, *[muffled in his cloak]*

  Soft, who is this? 'Tis not my son, disguised?
DAME KITELY
  (*She spies her husband come: and runs to him*)
  Oh, sir, have I forestalled your honest market?
  Found your close walks? You stand amazed, now, do you?
  I' faith, I am glad, I have smoked you yet at last!   30
  Where is your jewel trow? In: come, let's see her—
  Fetch forth your housewife, dame—if she be fairer,
  In any honest judgement, than myself,
  I'll be content with it: but, she is change,
  She feeds you fat, she soothes your appetite,   35
  And you are well? Your wife, an honest woman,
  Is meat twice sod to you, sir? Oh, you treachour!

19 *Belike . . . shut* i.e. you keep a brothel
22 *tried* trustworthy (ironic)   29 *close* private
32 *housewife* i.e. the whore you procure for
34 *change* fickleness; also 'a change', and, possibly, a pun on
    'Change, Exchange (i.e. 'in the market')
35 *fat* profit; 'fat' also meant the last part of any merchandise to be
    unloaded from a ship by the porters
37 *twice sod* twice boiled: unpalatable
    treachour traitor

KNO'WELL
  She cannot counterfeit thus plausibly.
KITELY
  Out on thy more than strumpet's impudence!
  Steal'st thou thus to thy haunts? And, have I taken   40
  Thy bawd, and thee, and thy companion,
                              (*Pointing to* OLD KNO'WELL)
  This hoary-headed lecher, this old goat,
  Close at your villainy, and would'st thou 'scuse it,
  With this stale harlot's jest, accusing me?
  (*To him*) Oh, old incontinent, dost not thou shame,   45
  When all thy powers in chastity is spent,
  To have a mind so hot? And to entice,
  And feed th' enticements of a lustful woman?
DAME KITELY
  Out, I defy thee, I, dissembling wretch!
KITELY
  Defy me, strumpet. [*Indicates* CASH] Ask they pandar, here, 50
  Can he deny it? Or that wicked elder?
KNO'WELL
  Why, hear you, sir.
KITELY   Tut, tut, tut: never speak.
  Thy guilty conscience will discover thee.
KNO'WELL
  What lunacy is this, that haunts this man?
KITELY
  Well, good wife B–A–'–D, Cob's wife; and you,   55
  That make your husband such a hoddy-doddy;
  And you, young apple-squire; and old cuckold-maker;
  I'll ha' you every one before a justice:
  Nay, you shall answer it, I charge you go.
KNO'WELL
  Marry, with all my heart, sir: I go willingly.   60
  Though I do taste this as a trick, put on me,

s.d. [*Indicates Cash*] By Thomas, F1: 'By': 'referring to'
  56 *hoddy-doddy* snail, i.e. cuckold
  57 *apple-squire* whore's attendant; pandar

---

  46 *When . . . spent.* This is obscure, unless 'chastity' be taken to mean
    'lawful pleasures'; in this case 'spent' cannot mean 'wasted', as S
    glosses it, but rather 'used up'; however, Kitely may be projecting him-
    self into the falsely accused figure of Kno'well, and thus 'chastity' may
    be used in its true sense: i.e. Kitely does 'spend' his 'powers', his
    sexual energy, in narcissistic fantasies of jealous imaginings.
  55 *B–A–'–D.* Kitely spells the word out, punning on 'bawd' and 'bad':
    the third letter should probably be expressed as an emphatic pause.

To punish my impertinent search; and justly:
And half forgive my son, for the device.

KITELY

Come, will you go?

DAME KITELY   Go? To thy shame, believe it.

[Enter] COB

COB

Why, what's the matter, here? What's here to do?   65

KITELY

Oh, Cob, art thou come? I have been abused,
And i' thy house. Never was man so, wronged!

COB

'Slid, in my house? My Master Kitely? Who wrongs you in
my house?

KITELY

Marry, young lust in old; and old in young, here: 70
Thy wife's their bawd, here have I taken 'hem.

COB

How? Bawd? Is my house come to that? Am I preferred
thither? (*He falls upon his wife and beats her*) Did I charge
you to keep your doors shut, Is'bel? And do you let 'hem
open for all comers?   75

KNO'WELL

Friend, know some cause, before thou beat'st thy wife,
This's madness, in thee.

COB   Why? Is there no cause?

KITELY

Yes, I'll show cause before the Justice, Cob:
Come, let her go with me.

COB   Nay, she shall go.

TIB

Nay, I will go. I'll see, an' you may be allowed to make a   80
bundle o' hemp, o' your right and lawful wife thus, at every
cuckoldly knave's pleasure. Why do you not go?

KITELY

A bitter quean. Come, we'll ha' you tamed.   *[Exeunt]*

---

83 *quean* whore

---

67 *so,* The comma indicates a pause while the most indignant word
   is sought.
72–73 *Am I preferred thither?* 'Have I been promoted to a brothel keeper?';
   also, 'Has someone supplanted me?'.
81 *bundle o' hemp.* Hemp was beaten when it was being made into rope;
   prostitutes did this work in Bridewell.

Act IV, Scene [ix]

[A Street]

[Enter] BRAINWORM *[disguised as a city-sergeant]*

BRAINWORM
Well, of all my disguises, yet, now am I most like myself:
being in this sergeant's gown. A man of my present profession, never counterfeits, till he lays hold upon a debtor,
and says, he rests him, for then he brings him to all manner
of unrest. A kind of little kings we are, bearing the diminutive   5
of a mace, made like a young artichoke, that always carries
pepper and salt, in itself. Well, I know not what danger I
undergo, by this exploit, pray heaven, I come well off.

[Enter] MATTHEW *[and]* BOBADILL

MATTHEW
See, I think, yonder is the varlet, by his gown.
BOBADILL
Let's go, in quest of him.   10
MATTHEW
'Save you, friend, are you not here, by appointment of
Justice Clement's man?
BRAINWORM
Yes, an't please you, sir: he told me two gentlemen had
willed him to procure a warrant from his master, which I
have about me, to be served on one Downright.   15
MATTHEW
It is honestly done of you both; and see, where the party
comes, you must arrest: serve it upon him, quickly, afore he
be aware—
BOBADILL
Bear back, Master Matthew.

[Enter] STEPHEN *[in Downright's cloak]*

BRAINWORM
Master Downright, I arrest you, i' the Queen's name, and   20
must carry you afore a justice, by virtue of this warrant.
STEPHEN
Me, friend? I am no Downright, I, I am Master Stephen,
you do not well, to arrest me, I tell you, truly: I am in
nobody's bonds, nor books, I, would you should know it. A

Scene [ix] Scene xi in Ff
4 *rests* arrests, quibbled on here

---

6 *mace.* This was the badge of office of the officious and well-hated
figure of the city-sergeant or bailiff; 'mace' is also a spice, hence the pun.

plague on you heartily, for making me thus afraid afore my   25
time.

BRAINWORM

Why, now are you deceived, gentlemen?

BOBADILL

He wears such a cloak, and that deceived us: but see, here a
comes, indeed! This is he, officer.

[Enter] DOWNRIGHT

DOWNRIGHT

Why, how now, signior gull! Are you turned filcher of late?   30
Come, deliver my cloak.

STEPHEN

Your cloak, sir? I bought it, even now, in open market.

BRAINWORM

Master Downright, I have a warrant I must serve upon you,
procured by these two gentlemen.

DOWNRIGHT

These gentlemen? These rascals!   *[Raises his cudgel]*   35

BRAINWORM

Keep the peace, I charge you, in her Majesty's name.

DOWNRIGHT

I obey thee. What must I do, officer?

BRAINWORM

Go before Master Justice Clement, to answer what they can
object against you, sir. I will use you kindly, sir.

MATTHEW

Come, let's before, and make the Justice, Captain—   40

BOBADILL

The varlet's a tall man! Afore heaven!

[Exeunt MATTHEW *and* BOBADILL*]*

STEPHEN

Sir, I bought it, and I'll keep it.

DOWNRIGHT

You will.

STEPHEN

Ay, that I will.

DOWNRIGHT

Officer, there's thy fee, arrest him.   45

BRAINWORM

Master Stephen, I must arrest you.

28 *a* he
40 *make* prepare

25–26 *afore my time.* Stephen is feeling guilty about the stolen cloak.
41 *tall.* Brave: referring to Brainworm's bravery in arresting Downright.

STEPHEN
Arrest me, I scorn it. There, take your cloak, I'll none on't.
DOWNRIGHT
Nay, that shall not serve your turn, now, sir. Officer, I'll go
with thee, to the Justice's: bring him along.
STEPHEN
Why, is not here your cloak? What would you have?   50
DOWNRIGHT
I'll ha' you answer it, sir.
BRAINWORM
Sir, I'll take your word; and this gentleman's, too: for his
appearance.
DOWNRIGHT
I'll ha' no words taken. Bring him along.
BRAINWORM
Sir, I may choose, to do that: I may take bail.   55
DOWNRIGHT
'Tis true, you may take bail, and choose; at another time:
but you shall not, now, varlet. Bring him along, or I'll swinge
you.   [*Raises cudgel*]
BRAINWORM
Sir, I pity the gentleman's case. Here's your money again.
DOWNRIGHT
'Sdeins, tell not me of my money, bring him away, I say.   60
BRAINWORM
I warrant you he will go with you of himself, sir.
DOWNRIGHT
Yet more ado?
BRAINWORM
[*Aside*] I have made a fair mash on't.
STEPHEN
Must I go?
BRAINWORM
I know no remedy, Master Stephen.   65
DOWNRIGHT
Come along, afore me, here. I do not love your hanging look
behind.
STEPHEN
Why sir. I hope you cannot hang me for it. Can he, fellow?
BRAINWORM
I think not, sir. It is but a whipping matter, sure.
STEPHEN
Why, then, let him do his worst, I am resolute.   [*Exeunt*]   70

Act V, Scene i

[*Coleman Street. A Hall in* JUSTICE CLEMENT'S *House*]

[*Enter*] CLEMENT, KNO'WELL, KITELY, DAME KITELY, TIB, CASH,
COB [*and*] SERVANTS

CLEMENT
Nay, but stay, stay, give me leave: my chair, sirrah. You,
Master Kno'well, say you went thither to meet your son.
KNO'WELL
Ay, sir.
CLEMENT
But, who directed you, thither?
KNO'WELL
That did mine own man, sir.   5
CLEMENT
Where is he?
KNO'WELL
Nay, I know not, now; I left him with your clerk: and
appointed him, to stay here for me.
CLEMENT
My clerk? About what time, was this?
KNO'WELL
Marry, between one and two, as I take it.   10
CLEMENT
And, what time came my man with the false message to you,
Master Kitely?
KITELY
After two, sir.
CLEMENT
Very good: but, Mistress Kitely, how that you were at Cob's?
Ha?   15
DAME KITELY
An' please you, sir, I'll tell you: my brother, Wellbred,
told me, that Cob's house, was a suspected place—
CLEMENT
So it appears, methinks: but, on.
DAME KITELY
And that my husband used thither, daily.
CLEMENT
No matter, so he used himself well, mistress.   20
DAME KITELY
True sir, but you know, what grows, by such haunts, often-
times.

21 *grows* comes to pass; but, of course, a pun

CLEMENT

I see, rank fruits of a jealous brain, Mistress Kitely: but,
did you find your husband there, in that case, as you suspected?   25

KITELY

I found her there, sir.

CLEMENT

Did you so? That alters the case. Who gave you knowledge,
of your wife's being there.

KITELY

Marry, that did my brother Wellbred.

CLEMENT

How? Wellbred first tell her? Then tell you, after? Where   30
is Wellbred?

KITELY

Gone with my sister, sir, I know not whither.

CLEMENT

Why, this is a mere trick, a device; you are gulled in this
most grossly, all! Alas, poor wench, wert thou beaten for
this?   35

TIB

Yes, most pitifully, and't please you.

COB

And worthily, I hope: if it shall prove so.

CLEMENT

Ay, that's like, and a piece of a sentence.

[*Enter a* SERVANT]

How now, sir? What's the matter?

SERVANT

Sir, there's a gentleman, i' the court without, desires to speak   40
with your worship.

CLEMENT

A gentleman? What's he?

SERVANT

A soldier, sir, he says.

---

29 *Marry . . . Wellbred.* A good deal of unnecessary fuss has been made
about how Kitely knew this, or how Clement knew that Dame Kitely had
been told; Q is clearer on the matter, so Jonson has been accused of
'loose plotting' in his revision: but it can all be explained by the conversation that has taken place off-stage both between Kitely and his
wife, and between them and Clement.

38 *a piece of a sentence.* Refers with facetious approval to Cob's mechanical
'if it shall prove so': i.e. the law cannot judge until it has heard the
whole story.

CLEMENT

A soldier? Take down my armour, my sword, quickly: a
soldier speak with me! Why, when knaves? (*He arms himself*)   45
Come on, come on, hold my cap there, so; give me my
gorget, my sword: stand by, I will end your matters, anon—
Let the soldier enter. ([*Enter*] BOBADILL [*and*] MATTHEW
[*Exit* SERVANT]) Now, sir what ha' you to say to me?

BOBADILL

By your worship's favour—   50

CLEMENT

Nay, keep out, sir, I know not your pretence, you send me
word, sir, you are a soldier: why, sir, you shall be answered,
here, here be them have been amongst soldiers. Sir, your
pleasure.

BOBADILL

Faith, sir, so it is, this gentleman, and myself, have been   55
most uncivilly wronged, and beaten, by one Downright, a
coarse fellow, about the town, here, and for mine own part,
I protest, being a man, in no sort, given to this filthy
humour of quarrelling, he hath assaulted me in the way of
my peace; despoiled me of mine honour; disarmed me of my   60
weapons; and rudely, laid me along, in the open streets:
when, I not so much as once offered to resist him.

CLEMENT

Oh, God's precious! Is this the soldier? Here, take my
armour off quickly, 'twill make him swoon, I fear; he is not
fit to look on't, that will put up a blow.   65

MATTHEW

An't please your worship, he was bound to the peace.

CLEMENT

Why, and he were, sir, his hands were not bound, were they?

[Enter SERVANT]

SERVANT

There's one of the varlets of the city, sir, has brought two
gentlemen, here, one, upon your worship's warrant.

CLEMENT

My warrant?   70

SERVANT

Yes, sir. The officer says, procured by these two.

---

47 *gorget* neck-armour; probably seldom actually used
50 begins Scene ii in Ff
51 *pretence* purpose
61 *laid me along* prostrated me

CLEMENT

Bid him, come in. [*Exit* SERVANT] Set by this picture. ([*Enter*] DOWNRIGHT, STEPHEN [*and*] BRAINWORM [*disguised as a city sergeant*]) What, Master Downright! Are you brought at Master Freshwater's suit, here?   75

DOWNRIGHT

I' faith, sir. And here's another brought at my suit.

CLEMENT

What are you, sir?

STEPHEN

A gentleman, sir. Oh, uncle!

CLEMENT

Uncle? Who? Master Kno'well.

KNO'WELL

Ay, sir! This is a wise kinsman of mine.   80

STEPHEN

God's my witness, uncle, I am wronged here monstrously, he charges me with stealing of his cloak, and would I might never stir, if I did not find it in the street, by chance.

DOWNRIGHT

Oh, did you find it, now? You said, you bought it, erewhile.

STEPHEN

And, you said, I stole it; nay, now my uncle is here, I'll do   85
well enough, with you.

CLEMENT

Well, let this breathe a while; you, that have cause to complain, there, stand forth: had you my warrant for this gentleman's apprehension?

BOBADILL

Ay, an't please your worship.   90

CLEMENT

Nay, do not speak in passion so: where had you it?

BOBADILL

Of your clerk, sir.

CLEMENT

That's well! An' my clerk can make warrants, and my hand not at 'hem! Where is the warrant? Officer, have you it?

BRAINWORM

No, sir, your worship's man, Master Formal, bid me do it,   95
for these gentlemen, and he would be my discharge.

74 Begins Scene iii in Ff. The entrance of Downright, Stephen and
     Brainworm is given at the end of Clement's speech
75 *Freshwater's* a freshwater soldier was one without experience
80 *wise* ironic
91 *in passion so* so sorrowfully

72 *picture.* i.e. Bobadill, who is only a picture of a soldier.

CLEMENT

Why, Master Downright, are you such a novice, to be
served, and never see the warrant?

DOWNRIGHT

Sir. He did not serve it on me.

CLEMENT

No? How then?   100

DOWNRIGHT

Marry, sir, he came to me, and said, he must serve it, and he
would use me kindly, and so—

CLEMENT

Oh, God's pity, was it so, sir? He must serve it? Give me my
long-sword there, and help me off; so. Come on, sir varlet,
I must cut off your legs, sirrah ([BRAINWORM *kneels*;] *he*   105
flourishes over him with his long-sword): nay, stand up, I'll
use you kindly; I must cut off your legs, I say.

BRAINWORM

[*Kneeling again*] Oh, good sir, I beseech you; nay, good
Master Justice.

CLEMENT

I must do it; there is no remedy. I *must* cut off your legs,   110
sirrah, I must cut off your ears, you rascal, I must do it; I
must cut off your nose, I must cut off your head.

BRAINWORM

Oh, good your worship.

CLEMENT

Well, rise, how dost thou do, now? Dost thou feel thyself
well? Hast thou no harm?   115

BRAINWORM

No, I thank your good worship, sir.

CLEMENT

Why, so! I said, I must cut off thy legs, and I must cut off
thy arms, and I must cut off thy head; but, I did not do it:
so, you said, you must serve this gentleman, with my
warrant, but, you did not serve him. You knave, you slave,   120
you rogue, do you say you must? Sirrah, away with him, to
the jail, I'll teach you a trick, for your *must*, sir.

BRAINWORM

Good sir, I beseech you, be good to me.

CLEMENT

Tell him he shall to the jail, away with him, I say.

BRAINWORM

Nay, sir, if you will commit me, it shall be for committing   125
more than this: I will not lose, by my travail, any grain of
my fame certain.   [*Throws off his disguise*]

CLEMENT
How is this!
KNO'WELL
My man, Brainworm!
STEPHEN
Oh yes, uncle. Brainworm has been with my cousin Edward, 130
and I, all this day.
CLEMENT
I told you all, there was some device!
BRAINWORM
Nay, excellent Justice, since I have laid myself thus open to
you; now, stand strong for me: both with your sword, and
your balance. 135
CLEMENT
Body o' me, a merry knave! Give me a bowl of sack: if he
belong to you, Master Kno'well, I bespeak your patience.
BRAINWORM
That is it, I have most need of. Sir, if you'll pardon me,
only; I'll glory in all the rest, of my exploits.
KNO'WELL
Sir, you know, I love not to have my favours come hard, 140
from me. You have your pardon: though I suspect you
shrewdly for being of counsel with my son, against me.
BRAINWORM
Yes, faith, I have, sir; though you retained me doubly this
morning, for yourself: first, as Brainworm; after, as
Fitzsword. I was your reformed soldier, sir. 'Twas I sent 145
you to Cob's, upon the errand, without end.
KNO'WELL
Is it possible! Or that thou should'st disguise thy language
so, as I should not know thee?
BRAINWORM
Oh, sir, this has been the day of my metamorphosis! It is
not that shape alone, that I have run through, today. I 150
brought this gentleman, Master Kitely, a message too, in the
form of Master Justice's man, here, to draw him out o' the
way, as well as your worship: while Master Wellbred might
make a conveyance of Mistress Bridget, to my young master.
KITELY
How! My sister stol'n away? 155
KNO'WELL
My son is not married, I hope!
BRAINWORM
Faith, sir, they are both as sure as love, a priest, and three

134–135 *sword . . . balance* both, somewhat ironically, emblems of
justice

thousand pound, which is her portion, can make 'hem: and
by this time are ready to bespeak their wedding supper at
the Windmill, except some friend, here, prevent 'hem, and   160
invite 'hem home.

CLEMENT

Marry, that will I. I thank thee, for putting me in mind on't.
Sirrah, go you, and fetch 'hem hither, upon my warrant.
Neither's friends have cause to be sorry, if I know the
young couple, aright. Here, I drink to thee, for thy good   165
news. But, I pray thee, what hast thou done with my man
Formal?

BRAINWORM

Faith, sir, after some ceremony past, as making him drunk,
first with story, and then with wine—but all in kindness—
and stripping him to his shirt: I left him in that cool vain,   170
departed, sold your worship's warrant to these two, pawned
his livery for that varlet's gown, to serve it in; and thus have
brought myself, by my activity, to your worship's con-
sideration.

CLEMENT

And I will consider thee, in another cup of sack. Here's to   175
thee, which having drunk off, this is my sentence. Pledge me.
Thou hast done, or assisted to nothing, in my judgement, but
deserves to be pardoned for the wit o' the offence. If thy
master, or any man, here, be angry with thee, I shall suspect
his ingine, while I know him for't. How now? What noise   180
is that?

[*Enter* SERVANT]

SERVANT

Sir, it is Roger come home.

CLEMENT

Bring him in, bring him in.

[*Enter*] FORMAL [*in a suit of armour*]

What! Drunk in arms, against me? Your reason, your reason
for this.   185

FORMAL

I beseech your worship to pardon me; I happened into ill
company by chance, that cast me into a sleep, and stripped
me of all my clothes—

CLEMENT

Well, tell him, I am Justice Clement, and do pardon him:
but, what is this to your armour! What may that signify?   190

160 *prevent* anticipate
180 *ingine* wit
182 begins Scene iv in Ff

FORMAL

And't please you, sir, it hung up i' the room, where I was
stripped; and I borrowed it of one o' the drawers, to come
home in, because I was loath, to do penance through the
street, i' my shirt.

CLEMENT

Well, stand by a while.   195

[*Enter*] ED. KNO'WELL, WELLBRED, [*and*] BRIDGET

Who be these? Oh, the young company, welcome, welcome.
Gi' you joy. Nay, Mistress Bridget, blush not; you are not
so fresh a bride, but the news of it is come hither afore you.
Master Bridegroom, I ha' made your peace, give me your
hand: so will I for all the rest, ere you forsake my roof.   200

ED. KNO'WELL

We are the more bound to your humanity, sir.

CLEMENT

Only these two, have so little of man in 'hem, they are no
part of my care.

WELLBRED

Yes, sir, let me pray you for this gentleman, he belongs, to
my sister, the bride.   205

CLEMENT

In what place, sir?

WELLBRED

Of her delight, sir, below the stairs, and in public: her *poet*,
sir.

CLEMENT

A *poet*? I will challenge him myself, presently, at *extempore*.
   Mount up thy Phlegon muse, and testify,   210
    How Saturn, sitting in an ebon cloud,
   Disrobed his podex white as ivory,
    And, through the welkin, thundered all aloud.

WELLBRED

He is not for *extempore*, sir. He is all for the pocket-muse,
please you command a sight of it.   215

202 *these two* Bobadill and Matthew
207 *below the stairs* i.e. as a menial, with an ironic sexual quibble
210–213 *Mount . . . cloud* this sounds like a parody, but no original
    has been traced
    Phlegon one of the horses of the Sun
214 *pocket-muse* 'he has poems already written out, in his pocket'

---

196 Begins Scene v in Ff. The entrance of Ed. Kno'well, Wellbred and
    Bridget is given after the end of Clement's speech.

CLEMENT

Yes, yes, search him for a taste of his vein.

[*They search* MATTHEW'S *pockets*]

WELLBRED

You must not deny the Queen's Justice, sir, under a writ o'
rebellion.

CLEMENT

What! All this verse? Body o' me, he carries a whole realm,
a commonwealth of paper, in's hose! Let's see some of his   220
subjects!

> *Unto the boundless Ocean of thy face,*
> *Runs this poor river charged with streams of eyes.*

How? This is stol'n.

ED. KNO'WELL

A parody! A parody! With a kind of miraculous gift, to   225
make it absurder than it was.

CLEMENT

Is all the rest, of this batch? Bring me a torch; lay it
together, and give fire. Cleanse the air. Here was enough to
have infected, the whole city, if it had not been taken in
time! See, see, how our *Poet's* glory shines! Brighter and   230
brighter! Still it increases! Oh, now, it's at the highest:
and, now, it declines as fast. You may see. *Sic transit gloria*
mundi.

KNO'WELL

There's an emblem for you, son, and your studies!

CLEMENT

Nay, no speech, or act of mine be drawn against such, as   235
profess it worthily. They are not born every year, as an
alderman. There goes more to the making of a good poet,
than a sheriff, Master Kitely. You look upon me! Though,
I live i' the city here, amongst you, I will do more reverence,
to him, when I meet him, than I will to the major, out of his   240

219 *realm* written and pronounced 'ream' (480 sheets of paper)
227 *Is . . . batch?* 'Are the rest as bad as these?'
232–233 *Sic . . . mundi* 'so passes away the glory of this world'

222–223 *Unto . . . eyes.* A burlesque of the first sonnet of Daniel's *Delia*
(1592). In Q the first four lines are quoted directly, and Matthew
mentions *Delia.*

234 *emblem.* A picture with a short poem explaining it: Kno'well imagines
that Clement shares his view of all poetry.

236–237 *They . . . aldermen.* One of Jonson's favourite maxims, adapted
from Florus, *De Qualitate Vitae*: 'Consules fiunt quotannis, et novi
proconsules,/solus aut rex aut poeta non quotannis nascitur': 'consuls
and proconsuls are renewed every year; only a king or a poet is not
born every year'.

year. But, these paper-pedlars! These ink-dabblers! They
cannot expect reprehension, or reproach. They have it with
the fact.

ED. KNO'WELL

Sir, you have saved me the labour of a defence.

CLEMENT

It shall be discourse for supper; between your father and   245
me, if he dare undertake me. But, to dispatch away these,
you sign o' the soldier, and picture o' the poet—but, both
so false, I will not ha' you hanged out at my door till
midnight—while we are at supper, you two shall penitently
fast it in my court, without; and, if you will, you may pray   250
there, that we may be so merry within, as to forgive, or
forget you, when we come out. Here's a third, because, we
tender your safety, shall watch you, he is provided for the
purpose. Look to your charge, sir.

STEPHEN

And what shall I do?   255

CLEMENT

Oh! I had lost a sheep, an he had not bleated! Why, sir,
you shall give Master Downright his cloak: and I will
entreat him to take it. A trencher, and a napkin, you shall
have, i' the buttery, and keep Cob, and his wife company,
here; whom, I will entreat first to be reconciled: and you to   260
endeavour with your wit, to keep 'hem so.

STEPHEN

I'll do my best.

COB

Why, now I see thou art honest, Tib, I receive thee as my
dear, and mortal wife, again.

TIB

And, I you, as my loving, and obedient husband.   265

CLEMENT

Good complement! It will be their bridal night, too. They
are married anew. Come, I conjure the rest, to put off all
discontent. You, Master Downright, your anger; you,
Master Kno'well, your cares; Master Kitely, and his wife,
their jealousy.   270

---

244 *Sir . . . defence* in Q this is made, at some length: see Intro-
    duction, p. xxix
252 *a third* Formal

242–243 *They . . . fact.* 'They are damned by what they are'.
264 *mortal.* As S suggests, Cob probably means 'moral'; Tib certainly
    means 'obedient' in her reply.

'For, I must tell you both, while that is fed,
Horns i' the mind are worse than o' the head'.

KITELY

Sir, thus they go from me, kiss me, sweetheart.

    'See what a drove of horns fly, in the air,
    Winged with my cleansed, and my credulous breath!   275
    Watch 'hem, suspicious eyes, watch, where they fall.
    See, see! On heads, that think they've none at all!
    Oh, what a plenteous world of this, will come!
    When air rains horns, all may be sure of some'.

I ha' learned so much verse out of a jealous man's part, in a   280
play.

CLEMENT

'Tis well, 'tis well! This night we'll dedicate to friendship,
love, and laughter. Master bridegroom, take your bride, and
lead; every one, a fellow. Here is my mistress—Brainworm!
To whom all my addresses of courtship shall have their   285
reference. Whose adventures, this day, when our grand-
children shall hear to be made a fable, I doubt not, but it shall
find both spectators, and applause.

THE END

271–279 *For . . . some.* The lines have not been traced, but the thought
expressed was a commonplace one.

*Made and printed in Great Britain by The Garden City Press Limited
Letchworth, Hertfordshire*